WIDE AWAKE IN DREAMLAND

Also by Michael Harrington

Porcupines at the Dance
Touched by the Dragon's Breath

WIDE AWAKE IN DREAMLAND

A Journey Ends at Colliding Rivers

MICHAEL HARRINGTON

Susan Creek Books
Wilsonville, Oregon

WIDE AWAKE IN DREAMLAND
A Journey Ends at Colliding Rivers

Copyright 2012, Michael Harrington

First Edition—2012

Cover image by Eva-Maria Schoen (Eva Shari)
Cover design by M. Harrington (with Barry Mack)
Editing by Karla Joy McMechan
Typesetting by Robin McBride

ISBN: 978-0-9748716-2-2
LCCN: 2012941327

Susan Creek Books
29030 SW Town Center Loop E.
Suite 202-250
Wilsonville, OR 97070
(503) 516-1106
www.SusanCreek.com

Dedication

To John Redstone, the Chief

To the company of actors who have
played their roles so magnificently in this
Dreamland Production called "Life."

Table of Contents

Preface

Thoreau sought to examine life, to drive it into a corner and reduce it to its basic elements, then publish what he found to the world. Conversely, I initially set out to write this book for my own edification. Only later did I discover the real reason for writing it.

Wide Awake in Dreamland's first notes were an attempt to clarify my understanding of the holographic nature of reality. My fascination with the light wave of creation and the Golden Thread, topics covered extensively in *Touched by the Dragon's Breath,*[1] followed closely on the heels of my study of synchronicity and waking dreams.[2] Both led me indirectly to this current topic.

After recently exploring the subjects of 2012 and the End-Time phenomenon, something began to bother me: Why did all the so-called authorities propound significantly different endings to this cosmic drama? If we were all living in the same reality field, wouldn't a common theme begin to emerge as we approached the finish line? Asking the right questions, augmented by my earlier studies, led me to the mystery of what I refer to as "the hologram."

By the time I had finished the rough outline for this book, I was struck by the realization that writing it would be unnecessary. By contemplating the holographic nature of reality, or what some call our "Reality Matrix," I was able to discover the reason why experts would likely disagree about our future. Furthermore, I came to peace with my prediction of a coming Golden Age that I'd summarized in *Dragon's Breath*. That being said, then why did I proceed with the writing of this book? I can think of only one reason: Because you asked me to.

—Michael Harrington
July, 2012

Introduction

I've come to the realization that I live in a sophisticated hologram designed to give the illusion of reality. For some time I had suspected that an absolute, "the same for everyone," outer world did not exist; but only recently have I actually come to *know* this. Evidently someone wanted me to discover this fact, for along my journey I've found hints and strategically placed signposts on numerous occasions.

The answer to the question posed in the Preface—why experts would disagree—came in a watershed realization: *"The* universe" does not exist. There is only *"my* universe" and, I assume, *"other people's* universes."

One day an obvious question struck me from out of the blue. It fit in with my contemplations of the hologram. How can I possibly know what is going on in someone else's universe? They, or their facsimiles, are only here in my holographic world playing roles that I have requested of them. I should interject here that this question was obvious only because I'd had a startling moment of awakening a few days before. I'll relate that "one with the universe" experience in detail in the proper sequence (Chapter Nine); but for now, I'll share the "Three Theaters" analogy that came out of it.

Imagine that a light is projecting outward from the center of your own being. You *are* this light. The film passing through the light carries images. These images are projected as physical events upon a spherical theater screen surrounding a 3D likeness of yourself. From your vantage point, you are the center of the universe. But more importantly, everything in your universe, your hologram, is also you. It is made from your light.

Your two friends, the ones you have coffee with every morning, in all likelihood are projecting their own universes in their respective theaters, as well. You may never know, for the only thing you will ever know for sure is how your friends play the roles you have asked them to play in your universe. Do you see? The only thing you'll know about me, this writer, is how I fulfilled my role in my brief appearance in your play.

The storyline for the movie currently playing in your theater is influenced by the "consensus reality" of all the players in the world drama at this time. As everything is intimately connected at a deeper level, the plot shifts and turns as the actors intermingle and play their roles with either love or fear. A small number of players can influence the plot through the hundredth-monkey principle.

Each slice of a hologram, no matter how thin, contains everything present in the whole. Sticking with our movie analogy, similar versions of the same script may be playing in every theater in the world. Since it appears as if we're all viewing the same movie from slightly different perspectives, we mistakenly assume that we're all in same theater.

So you can now see why none of the authorities will ever completely agree on the ending to this drama, and it *is* a drama in my theater, not a comedy, although it has its moments. It is likely that we're all projecting a similar version of the same movie, sending facsimiles of ourselves into each other's theaters to play the roles we agreed upon before this life. But I can't say this with certainty, because I can only know what is going on in the hologram I'm now projecting. Anything outside of this is pure speculation.

To recap, everything you see about you is made of your light, it *is* you. You are both creating and experiencing your own hologram, as am I. If you can grasp this principle, you may not need to read any further. This may be all my cameo appearance in your play or movie was all about.

While I was reluctant to write about personal experiences, I soon discovered that it would be necessary in order to adequately examine the hologram (see *Part I: Perchance to Dream*). Some memories were fun to revisit, others quite painful, but all were a part of the awakening process.

Many have asked, "Whatever happened to the Chief?" the friend and mentor I wrote about in *Porcupines at the Dance*[1] and *Dragon's Breath*. Part of this book is dedicated to answering that question and to memorializing our final conversations (*Part II: The Chief's Final Discourses*). These discussions included the key to invincibility, the mechanics of the hologram, the Hero's Journey, and the path to the heart.

The final section of the book (*Part III: A Holographic View of the End Times*) features three intriguing topics: "The Seven-Year Window" made famous by the

Mayans, our arrival at "Zero Point," and lastly, what I consider to be the two most likely alternate finales to the End-Times movie. As creator-beings we wield immense power. Our light and God's Light are one and the same. Beliefs and expectations carry a lot of weight in determining our experiences in the hologram, including those looming just ahead.

Of course, ultimately, it may be our Higher Selves who choose which version we experience here in "Dreamland." I know that my Higher Self fancies himself as a writer, too, and may see me simply as a beloved, yet expendable, character in this fascinating movie.

PART ONE

Perchance to Dream

"To be awake is to be alive. I have
never yet met a man who was quite
awake. How could I have looked him
in the face?"
—Henry David Thoreau
Walden (1854)[1]

–1–

Stan, Stan, the Bigfoot Man

Had I realized at a younger age that I live in a hologram, would I have taken life less seriously? That was the question *du jour* on the morning I set off for Colliding Rivers, at least one of them. I'd caught glimpses of the holographic nature of reality from time to time, but these tantalizing morsels had only whetted my appetite. I was hungry for more.

Every adventure should begin with three things: a good cup of coffee, a question, and a song. This trip to Colliding Rivers in the spring of 2001 was no exception; but it began with *two* questions. Although I rarely drink coffee today, on that chilly March morning that first sip must have tasted especially good. It was probably my imagination, but just holding a steaming cup of coffee helped clarify my thoughts when pondering deeper subjects than usual, like the hologram.

That no two people experience the same reality was apparent to me, but I had yet to fully understand why. This trip was timely. The man I was going to meet was an expert on the mechanics of creation.

The second question that morning was simply, "why?" A letter had come two weeks earlier requesting my presence at Colliding Rivers on this very Saturday. I knew the reason. I was to meet John Redstone, the Chief, a dear friend and mentor. But why had the letter come from a woman named Marilyn? Why hadn't the Chief contacted me himself?

Several months earlier he had called me from out of the blue. I was surprised to hear that he'd been living in a bedroom community of Portland, less than an hour away. We had talked about meeting for lunch, but I'd failed to follow through with a day and time. Perhaps the Chief had taken it upon himself to plan a reunion with this mysterious invitation.

Oh, the name on the letter was familiar. Mr. Redstone had mentioned Marilyn Waters on several occasions and I'd seen photos of them together. I had always wanted to meet her in person. The petite, dark-haired woman had been a prominent person in the Chief's life when he'd been young. He had spoken of her often with great affection. I was pleased to hear that she was now back in his life. Soon enough I'd have my answers, I reassured myself. I flipped on the radio and settled back in my seat for the three-hour drive from Portland to Colliding Rivers.

The Song and Hoyt

It was synchronistically appropriate that the first words out of the speakers were familiar: "Jeremiah was a bullfrog, was a good friend of mine. . . ." Few people realize that this Three Dog Night song has ties with Colliding Rivers. A famous songwriter used to live just north of Glide in a log cabin overlooking the

North Umpqua River. His mom got the family business of songwriting started when she wrote a hit for Elvis called "Heartbreak Hotel."

Her grown son, Hoyt, used to invite a few local kids over to his cabin while he strummed his old guitar, testing his lyrics on his young critics. A friend of mine named Randy was one of this gang of ten-year-olds. One day Hoyt asked Randy and his friends what they thought of his newest composition, one about a bullfrog. They liked it a lot, and so did Three Dog Night. "Joy to the World" became a huge hit for them. Hoyt Axton lived in the area for several years before divorcing and moving closer to the bright lights of the entertainment world.

Hoyt was probably the most famous celebrity living near Colliding Rivers. But having never met him in person made him far less interesting to me than Stan, a retired logger who reportedly talked to Bigfoot.

Befriending Bigfoot

Even in my youth I believed that people experience different versions of reality. I didn't have a clue why this was so, but it gave me an open door to investigate things others would roll their eyes at. Perhaps it was only true in his reality, but I knew right away that Stan's story was legitimate. Both he and his wife came across as sincere; they exuded kindness and a simple goodness.

Once a month Stan held meetings at his house in the country to talk about his experiences with Bigfoot. He told me that he'd first seen Bigfoot a few years back while out hunting near his property. Stopping to rest in a clearing, Stan happened to glance out across the

5

brush and vine maple at an old stump. What he saw made his jaw drop. Resting his arms upon the top of the stump, supporting his head, was a Bigfoot. According to Stan, the stump was approximately seven feet tall.

From conversations I'd had with Stan, I surmised that he was very psychic. When I first heard Stan tell this story, I wondered if he'd seen Bigfoot with his physical eyes or with his inner vision. I never did answer that question to my satisfaction, but considering Bigfoot's use of trans-dimensional vortices, I suspect that he was both a physical being and a multidimensional one.

When the Bigfoot saw Stan staring in his direction holding a deer rifle, he stood motionless, but without fear. Stan slowly lowered his gun, then placed it on the ground at his feet. He began to speak in a soft voice, explaining to the Bigfoot that he meant him no harm. Stan said that he just wanted to give him love.

Stan told the Bigfoot that he would come back to the same clearing the following day. He would leave his gun at home. If the Bigfoot wanted to communicate, then he should return about the same time. The next day Stan arrived at the meadow expecting to find it empty. But there, leaning against the very same stump, was the Bigfoot. Stan began to communicate telepathically. He told him about his home, and what he had loved about working in the woods falling timber. Stan told him about his wife and children, his hobbies, and his beliefs. The Bigfoot stood motionless, Stan related, focusing intently on the human standing before him.

That first meeting didn't last long. The Bigfoot walked off into the forest and disappeared from view. Over the course of several weeks, however, Stan encountered the Bigfoot on numerous occasions, mostly near the clearing where they'd initially met. He would speak, and then wait for the telepathic reply. A trust was established.

According to Stan, litle by little the Bigfoot began to communicate about his own life. There were small families of Bigfoot People living in remote areas in Oregon, Washington, and northern California near Mt. Shasta. This Bigfoot's family lived close by. They'd been residing in the area for many years. The Bigfoot People had taken common last names, like the "Johnson clan."

One summer afternoon the Bigfoot took Stan into the forest where he lived with his family. Stan was accepted by them and spent the night in the forest getting acquainted. He didn't go into detail about the Bigfoot's personal life and became quite evasive when asked about the location of his wood and stone dwelling. When I questioned him about the family, Stan would only say how accomodating and kind they had been. One child, about six feet tall, lived with the Bigfoot and his mate.

The Vortex

Perhaps the most remarkable part of Stan's story was the mysterious vortex. He told me how to find it once, never suspecting that I'd get within a hundred miles of it. But I followed his directions and found a spot about fifty feet off the side of an old logging road, not far from Stan's house. The air felt electrically charged. Oh, I was tempted to step into the portal, but there were too many unanswered questions: What would happen, if anything? Where did it lead? Was there a door on the other side? And the big one, What if I went through and couldn't get back?

But Stan had a guide. One evening the Bigfoot told Stan about the passage his people used to travel into the dimension just above this one. Whether it was a subplane of the Astral or a higher one, I can't say. The Bigfoot offered to take him through. There was just one catch. Stan would have to strip down to what Mother Nature had given him. His guide explained that anything metal would burn his skin in the process of passing through the vortex. Being rather modest, Stan refused to take off his briefs, which had a brass snap.

The Bigfoot stepped into the vortex and immediately disappeared. Summoning all his courage, Stan followed. He described feeling a tingling sensation, accompanied by a strange electrical pulse. Almost immediately he found himself standing on a perfectly manicured lawn. Not far away, a lion was grazing on tender shoots of grass. Stan explained that the vegetarian lion wasn't interested in dining on the new arrivals.

In the distance was a beautiful white castle set against the irridescent blue sky. Following the Bigfoot to the entrance, they were greeted by what could only be described as a fairy tale family, complete with a young girl dressed like a princess. Stan stayed in that land for several days; but upon returning through the vortex discovered that he'd only been gone about six hours.

At this point in retelling his story, Stan always brought out a photo his wife had taken the evening he'd returned from his adventure. There was a bright red burn mark on Stan's abdomen. It was the exact same size as the metal snap on his boxer briefs.

I give Stan a lot of credit for stepping into the vortex. As I said, after hearing his story I gave the matter some serious thought. One night I even camped out near the vortex. Before retiring, I placed a white pebble on top of a nearby stump as kind of a "get acquainted" gesture. The next morning the white stone was gone. I was excited to discover that my gift had been accepted, but mostly I was freaked out. While the idea of meeting a Bigfoot face to face was tantalizing, it was too big a step outside of my comfort zone. Would I do it now? Hmm.

Marina

Most of those visiting Stan were locals like me. However, one day when I was there, two older men and a young woman flew in from overseas. They'd come from one of the Scandinavian countries.

It was readily apparent that the two gentlemen were quite enamored of the lady, Marina, who looked to be in her early thirties. She stood approximately six feet tall, with shiny brown hair and big brown eyes. While listening in on their conversation, I detected a slight accent, but her command of the English language was remarkable.

That particular evening there was an excited buzz in the air. Rumor had it that the attractive young woman wasn't from Scandinavia at all. She was from a bit further away—a starship!

That was the only time Marina came to Stan's. Perhaps she had other stops to make in America. Perhaps she returned to wherever she came from. I never did ask. I couldn't help wondering, however, if she'd been here on a mission of sorts, observing, teaching, planning . . . perhaps laying the groundwork for some "contact event" in the distant future, perhaps around 2012. And most bewildering: Why had she chosen to travel to a small town in Oregon to visit a man who reportedly talked with Bigfoot? I hadn't a clue.

Even before meeting Marina, I would stare up at the stars at every opportunity. It goes without saying that I was a big fan of Captain Kirk, Spock, and later, Picard. The most intriguing part of Star Trek for me was the holodeck, the device that created a believable, artificial reality. Was the universe trying to teach me something through this show? Absolutely.

Sometimes after turning off the television I would imagine myself visiting other civilizations in far flung reaches of the universe. Life there had to be more exciting than it was on Earth, I speculated. But I was stuck here. Instead of alien encounters, I had schoolwork and chores. Passing from adolescence into adulthood, I found myself settling into a comfortable, yet predictable, routine much like those of my compatriots. An occasional trip to Colliding Rivers like this one today was a welcome change.

The Hologram's First Clues

A truck towing a trailer with two horses pulled into the rest area just north of Salem as I was stretching my back. A middle-aged woman wearing riding pants and a white sweatshirt walked past without looking over. Extras in movies have a purpose. In our own "holographic movies," I asked myself, What roles did people like the horse lady play? What purpose could this person possibly fulfill by appearing in my life for that brief instant? And what about the other people mingling about the rest area that I hadn't noticed?

Have you ever watched a movie a second time and focused on the extras in the background? Usually they're talking, eating, drinking, walking, or standing—all insignificant roles. But they add depth to the movie. Perhaps that's what the horse lady was doing, adding depth to my "rest stop scene." Or perhaps her horses held the key. In my world there was indeed a connection between horses and the hologram. Maybe it's true: Everything has meaning. Our lack of awareness just prevents us from seeing it.

While we were in junior high, a friend had brought some cards to school. They weren't playing cards; they had pictures of a single horse on them. The same horse was on every card, but the legs on each one were in slightly advanced positions. When the deck was fanned, the horse appeared to be running. The still images came to life. It was a crude motion picture.

When I first met John Redstone at Colliding Rivers, the man I affectionately called "The Chief," he had stated that the motion picture had been inspired by the light wave of creation. Ideas are expressed, then voided back to stillness so that another idea can be expressed in the next instant. This process takes place in a box called a "light wave." A chapter in *Dragon's Breath* is dedicated to this topic.[2] The Chief had also explained how the Golden Thread connects all light waves throughout the universe.

I don't recall for certain who had brought the horse cards to school, but Patrick springs to mind. We were friends throughout high school and worked at the plywood mill in town together for awhile. Patrick was only mildly interested in metaphysics, but he surprised me at times with his thoughtful observations.

One day he said something very strange. We were talking about imagination. I doubt that Patrick fully understood the significance of his remark. He told me that sometimes he imagined that he was the only living person in the universe. Everyone else in the world was just a cardboard cutout, an extra in his personal movie. The statement sounded totally bizarre at the time, but something told me to file it away in memory. It turned out to be a gold mine, one more clue as to the validity of the hologram.

Patrick loved playing pinball. He played it for hours. I gave pinball a token glance, but there was another arcade game that captured my attention. It was a road race game. I would stand in front of the machine holding a wheel that simulated an automobile steering wheel. Boulders and other obstacles would come flying by at lightening speed. It gave the illusion that I was actually driving a car down a winding road dodging hazards. After concentrating on the changing road conditions for several minutes, it was easy to forget that I was standing still and that the road race was going on in a tiny black box.

The road race game was the only one I really enjoyed. I played it over and over for a short time in my adolescent life. Later I realized that it had been my introduction to the hologram. The dream land I was living in was not radically different, only more sophisticated.

Around the time I was going to Stan's house, I met Angie, a charming woman who was also studying metaphysics. One day she told me an interesting story, one that reinforced my belief in "personal realities." Angie was at a metaphysical seminar, surrounded by a group of people who were talking informally during a break. On rare occasions, masters will appear to a person when they have critical information to pass on; but generally they prefer to teach in the dream state where the student is more receptive.

An adept walked up to Angie at the seminar and spoke briefly about a personal matter. She was surprised, of course, but also astounded that a master would risk disrupting a large group by making such an appearance. Afterward, Angie cautiously asked the people standing nearby if they had noticed anything unusual. But none had seen the royally dressed adept speaking with her. Angie's experience provided another confirmation that we live in completely individualized universes.

The Headliner

On vacation in Nevada I was shown firsthand yet another example of the holographic nature of reality. I had accompanied a friend to a stage show in Reno. The headliner was a well-known hypnotist. When she asked for volunteers from the audience, I raised my hand and was invited to come up on stage. A woman seated in the row behind me was also selected. Several attempts to put me under failed, but the woman turned out to be a prime candidate. [Had I known the dangers of hypnosis back then, I would never have volunteered to be a subject.]

After putting her under, the hypnotist walked the woman through several sensory experiences which apparently were real only to her. She smelled roses, saw cavalry on the horizon, and tasted both chocolate and rancid oysters, making the appropriate facial expressions for each.

At one point, the hypnotist gave the woman a pair of red shoes. These were the ones "she had always wanted." Her face lit up with joy. But then an invisible donkey was led on stage. "Oh, no," the hypnotist cried out, "that donkey just soiled your new shoes!"

The woman let out a horrified gasp and wrinkled up her nose. The hypnotist handed her an invisible rag and she began wiping off her beautiful red shoes. Of course the audience just roared. I was stunned into silence. What were the odds that we were all living in the exact same universe, I wondered? Probably not good.

The Missing Daughter

The most memorable case for the validity of individual realities comes from a book called *The Holographic Universe* by Michael Talbot.[3] In the mid 1970s the author's father hired a professional hypnotist to entertain a group of friends at his home. At one point during the night, the hypnotist successfully hypnotized a friend of his father's named Tom. The two had not met prior to the party.

Tom was then subjected to a number of tricks. He was made to believe that a giraffe was in the room, for example, and that a potato was really an apple, which he ate with gusto. Talbot writes that the highlight of the evening came when the hypnotist brought Tom out of the trance. Before doing so, however, he told Tom that, when he awoke, his teenage daughter, Laura, would be invisible to him.

With Laura standing directly in front of Tom's chair, the hypnotist asked, "Do you see your daughter?" Tom, now fully awake, looked around the room. His gaze appeared to pass right through his giggling daughter. "No," he replied, somewhat concerned. The hypnotist asked again (while Laura giggled), and once more Tom answered that he could not see her. Then came the most incredible part of the experience.

The hypnotist walked around behind Laura, apparently hidden from Tom's view, and pulled something from his pocket. Keeping it hidden from the rest of the guests, he pressed it against the small of the girl's back and asked Tom to identify what he saw.

Tom leaned toward his daughter's stomach, staring intently at something no one else could see. "A watch," he replied. Nodding, the hypnotist asked him if he could read the inscription. Tom leaned closer to his daughter, squinting to make out the writing, then correctly recited the name of the watch's owner and the inscription.

The hypnotist then passed the watch around the room to confirm what Tom had reported. Afterwards, Tom told Talbot that his daughter had been absolutely invisible to him. He had only seen the hypnotist standing alone holding the watch in his cupped hand. Talbot concludes, "Had the hypnotist let him leave the party without telling him what was going on he never would have known he wasn't perceiving normal consensus reality."

Skeptics might chime in at this point and say that Tom was a plant. I've found it difficult to convince nonbelievers that their versions of reality are lacking. On occasion, however, I did try. It's not easy admitting when you're wrong; but I now realize that I was wrong. Who was I to tell another person what was happening in his or her individual universe? My full-time job is trying to figure out what is happening in my own. And that, my friend, is quite often a mystery!

*   *   *

"Is *all* that we see or seem
but a dream within a dream?"
—Edgar Allan Poe
"A Dream within a
Dream" (1849)[4]

–2–

Crossing Kaiulani

Returning to Colliding Rivers always brings back vivid memories, mostly pleasant, a few, not so much. Driving is a form of therapy for me. With the conscious mind occupied, new perspectives on old issues often come through from the subconscious, as well as flashes of inspiration.

Remembering my experiences growing up in southern Oregon is one thing; writing about them is yet another. Since I've already filed away the memories, I didn't feel the need to revisit them on paper. But I was reminded that I'm not writing this book for myself.

Most would agree that returning to our old stomping grounds from time to time gives us pause for reflection. I suppose we all think our life is normal, at least in the beginning. At some point, however, we begin comparing our experiences with others and our opinion may change. When I was five I learned a surprising fact: not everyone is open to spiritual experiences.

Early Adventures in Dreamland

Growing up in the country at a quicksilver mine had its good points and bad. Later in life I ran into some health problems from exposure to the liquid metal. But as a kid, the setting provided ample opportunities for adventure and plenty of room to roam. Sometimes I'd watch the miners haul their trainloads of ore from the damp, dark tunnels. Occasionally I would get to ride on the train. The Bonanza Mine offered forty acres of rugged terrain to explore, as well.

Thankfully, I was given more freedom than most five-year-olds, and often became quite adventuresome in my travels about the property. Sometimes I'd leave home after lunch without returning until dusk. On my way home from one such outing, I stopped to catch my breath at the edge of a high mountain meadow sprinkled with bluebonnets and buttercups. The roof of our house was only a small dot upon the valley floor.

The last light of the sun was a dim glow above the distant hills as I stepped anxiously into the tranquil meadow. It would be dark soon. I'd always been home by this time. Suddenly a cold chill swept through me, interrupting my thoughts. Someone was standing near the center of the meadow, about forty yards away. I couldn't see him, but I could feel his powerful presence pervading the area. And I *knew* that he saw me!

"Be not afraid," his voice boomed. It was not a physical voice, but an impression that I heard inside my head. I bolted. Fate guided my footsteps through the fir and pine, but it was fear that made me run so fast.

My dad looked at me in silence as I told my story. His presence was comforting, but his answer upset me. He informed me that it had only been my imagination. I knew differently; but a part of me closed down that night. I learned that I could never speak of my encounters with the unknown, at least not with my father.

I was also aware of the "Little People" who danced through the fields of dandelions and strawberries near my house. While I couldn't actually see their colorful green, yellow, and red clothing, I saw it through "knowingness" without using my physical senses. I wanted to run with them through the flowers but something held me back. It was a doubt, planted by my father's lack of understanding. Even so, my experiences with the unknown continued.

A Near-Fatal Decision

In the mining of mercury, also known as quicksilver, the ore is put through a smeltering process. The intense heat frees the metal from the rock known as cinnabar. The leftover slag is then dumped into piles. Often I would wait for the slag train at the portal of the mine and ride out with the engineer, Bus Conn, as he dumped his cars.

There were two slag piles at the Bonanza Mine, both a hundred feet in height and several hundred yards long. The end of one sloped off gently, at a forty-five degree angle. Although it was forbidden, my five-year-old friend and I would jump off the end of the pile and slide to the bottom. My mom always wondered why my blue jeans wore out so quickly in the seat. It was great fun. But later I realized that we could have been buried alive.

The other pile, however, was no longer used. Time and erosion had turned this one into a hundred-foot cliff. Though I was born with an adventurous spirit, by nature I was a careful youth. But once in awhile my thirst for excitement would drive me beyond the edge.

One day my friend and I watched from the top as a pickup truck pulled away after filling his bed with slag below us. We decided to sail off the edge and slide down after it. We were twenty feet from the end, running full speed, when my friend suddenly stopped. I was airborne by the time I realized why. I'd jumped off the wrong pile, the hundred-foot cliff. Why had this truck been parked below the old one? The best rock was always in the new pile. Everybody knew that!

I looked down helplessly. All of a sudden I felt something around me. It felt like someone had wrapped his arms lightly around my waist, just enough to stop my forward momentum. Very calmly I spun in mid-air, catching the edge of the precipice with my fingertips. Effortlessly, I pulled myself to the top where my friend awaited anxiously.

"How did you do that?" he questioned. His eyes were wide. "You could have gotten yourself killed!" I couldn't answer him. Apparently someone was helping me, and I was pretty sure it wasn't just my imagination. But who? And why? There were rare times when I'd get the feeling that I was here for a reason, to learn something, or find something, but what?

One snowy evening, roughly three years later, I caught a glimpse of something beyond our physical reality deep in the woods. I'd been searching for a Christmas tree and had stopped to enjoy the scenery beside a crisp mountain stream. Behind a curtain of snowflakes I detected a presence. I heard a subtle, high-pitched sound emanating from an unknown source. It could have been my imagination, but I thought I saw a river of light flowing through the heavens. Deep inside I felt that I'd been privy to something very special, even sacred. Many years later I would learn that my assumption had been correct.

Sight without Eyes

One particular evening at the mine stands out in memory, perhaps because my thoughts that day had seemed totally foreign. I was around ten at the time, heading in for a late dinner after playing in the field with friends below our house. Before entering the porch I stopped abruptly. In a trance-like state, I gazed out across the meadow toward the top of the adjacent hill. A laurel tree stood watch from the summit, a stately guardian of the valley below.

The strangest thought popped into my head. I remember sitting down on the porch steps and closing my eyes. "I can know what's going on at the top of that hill without walking up there," I said to myself.

For several minutes I tried to visualize the view from that perspective. I attempted to read the initials kids had carved into the bark of the laurel. Was there activity in the next valley? A rancher had recently built a new barn. What did the wind feel like on the ridge? I could almost feel it brushing against my cheek. Were there birds on the branches? Could they see "me"? I tried to answer these questions in order to get the sensation of actually being there. My body surely would stay behind. But what part of me would be able to know what was happening on the summit?

Finally, after ten minutes of straining to "see without my eyes," I gave up and went inside. I was pretty disappointed that the images in my mind hadn't been clearer; they were only sketchy, black and white, "memory-like" pictures. "Someday I'll be able to do that," I vowed with determination, not understanding what "that" really was.

Out of the Body

When I was fourteen I had an experience that taught me that I was more than simply a physical body. Occasionally I'd feel my astral form, as I came to know it later, lift out of its physical container as I was drifting off to sleep. From above my bed I could look down and see the entire room quite clearly. The freedom was incredible.

But one night I panicked. I'd drifted out like before, then after a short tour of my room decided to get back in my body. It was curled up in a ball in the bed. But I couldn't sink back in. What would happen to the body if I couldn't return, I wondered? Even more important, what would happen to the real me? The sound of gentle laughter hit my consciousness, followed by welcome instructions: "You must assume the same position as the physical body in the bed." The advice from my unseen guardian worked perfectly. I was able to sink back in.

Summer School

With 8th grade now thankfully behind me, I was free from the rigors of study, or so I thought. But that first day of vacation ended with unsettling questions.

Shortly after turning in after a full day of play, a short, solidly built man silently appeared at my bedside. Taking my hand, we floated upward toward the ceiling on invisible wings. Once again, I could see my physical body lying motionless in the bed below. My guide offered no explanation, but smiled at my bewilderment as we passed right through the ceiling!

Continents passed beneath us as we traversed vast expanses of space, finally touching down on a snow-capped ridge. A remote monastery clung tenaciously to the side of the steep mountain. My guide escorted me across a wide, wooden walkway that led to a long hall with sturdy double doors. An oriental man, wearing a floor-length white robe, greeted us at the entrance. The two men spoke briefly, then, without looking over, my guide tipped his head sideways toward me. "He is here to learn," he told the abbot, then wheeled about and abruptly left.

I awoke the next morning remembering the abbot's kind demeanor as he had ushered me through the lighted door, but nothing more. I had no answers, but many questions: Who was the mysterious stranger who had taken me from my bed? What had I been taken there to learn? And why had I been singled out for this dubious honor? My reaction to the night's adventure was probably typical of most eighth graders. "What rotten luck," I complained. "Now I have to go to summer school!"

Some Answers Arrive

Seven years later, when I was twenty-one, a high school classmate pulled up in front of my house in his faded, red Volkswagen. He'd just returned from the service. A short article about "out-of-the-body travel" was taped to his back passenger-side window. It explained that one could consciously leave the body by practicing simple spiritual exercises. A host of grand adventures lay beyond our limited, waking consciousness. There were places where one could learn the history of our galaxy, for instance, or study esoteric wisdom. Myriad temples were scattered throughout the universe and higher dimensions for those who wished to learn. Memories of the white-robed abbot and my short, quiet guide came to mind.

The article also mentioned that a number of ascended masters had come to help the planet and humanity transition through an extended time of darkness.[1] They were here to help people wake up from the illusion, the hologram. Some had been historical figures in our past.

I remembered something from my childhood—an encounter in the woods—a question: What was that mystical, musical presence that had haunted me for years?

On my friend's back window I read about a wave of spiritual energy—pure love—that flowed out of the heart of God. It was called the "Sound Current," or "Audible Life Stream."[2] I would later learn that Pythagoras called it the "Music of the Spheres."[3] It belongs to no particular religion. By connecting with the returning wave, one can return with it to its Source.[4]

My friend told me that by repeating charged words, such as "HU," a secret name for God, it was possible to connect with this celestial current. Flashing lights went off in my head! I realized that I'd been searching for the Music of the Spheres since I'd been young. Its source lay beyond the illusion of Dreamland.

Comic Relief

Baseball played a big part in my adolescent life. Since my father had once been a professional scout, I'm certain he had dreams of seeing his two boys in major league uniforms. One evening he brought home a brand new pitching machine. It was an extravagant thing to buy considering his income at the time. But nothing was too good for his boys when it came to baseball. Since I was the youngest by nine years, my main duty was chasing down balls my brother would hit. I'd get in a few swings, but never enough for my satisfaction.

The sleek, shiny machine was never unplugged. It beckoned to me from its position on the flats below the slag pile. It taunted me. It knew I wasn't allowed to use it alone. Finally one evening I gave in to temptation.

I was a little intimidated by it at first. It looked so powerful sitting there at the highest setting, major league speed. Timidly, I flipped on the switch. I'd start at the top. I could hear the gears grinding menacingly behind me as I scurried back to home plate.

Will Rogers once remarked that everything is funny as long as it happens to somebody else. When the ball flew out of the machine it looked like a BB. At that very moment I discovered something quite disturbing: Someone had moved home plate. The ninety-mile-an-hour fastball hit me dead center in the middle of the back! But getting hit with things wasn't all that uncommon.

There was the time a friend and I had thrown bolts at a distant tank of water. I'd bent down in front of him to pick up a bolt, then stood up as he'd let one fly. If I wasn't being hit with a baseball or a bolt, it was only because I'd taken the wrong bus and was on my way to a more horrible fate yet.

Sharp objects were especially hazardous. My hand still bears a jagged scar from the day I nearly lost my thumb while slicing the end off a watermelon. Probably the most embarrassing incident involved a bow and arrow.

I'd patiently watched my neighbor from our porch as he repeatedly shot his round-pointed arrow into the heavens. I'd never owned a bow, but had always wanted one. At last my neighbor went inside for lunch. Nonchalantly I strolled across the field and picked up the bow. It was a nice one. I shot the arrow into the air, and then picked it up when it fell to earth nearby. Higher I shot it, and higher. I could almost shoot it out of sight. Then finally I did!

Not once did I think of what I'd do if I actually succeeded. I looked toward the sky, noticeably pleased with myself. Then, just like in the cartoons, my smile dimmed. I'd made one mistake already. I wasn't about to compound it by just standing there. I threw down the bow and ran. I'd gone about ten feet when the most amazing thing happened. The arrow came down and hit me right on top of the head!

Fortunately it was a glancing blow. It penetrated the knit cap I was wearing, missing my left ear by a fraction of an inch. I burst out laughing at the foolishness of my decision. No doubt the Guardian Angels and Ascended Masters called an emergency meeting that day to draw straws. Who would be the one to teach "William Tell" the secrets of the universe? First on the agenda: Better decisions.

Crossing Kaiulani

I made the decision to move to Hawaii when I was in my late twenties. It was a good one. The eight months I lived there were a complementary blend of poetry, spiritual studies, and an occasional Mai Tai. Although I've given up alcohol, that first Mai Tai on Waikiki Beach must have tasted especially good. But what I remember most about Hawaii was my first walk from the condo to the beach.

Many of the buildings and streets in Honolulu are named after past Hawaiian royalty. By the way, every vowel is pronounced in the Hawaiian language, but I can think of a couple of exceptions. When an "a" is followed by an "i," then the "a" is silent. Also, "au" is pronounced "ow;" so "Kau" would sound like "cow." It takes some getting used to.

That first day I bought some flip flops, some suntan lotion, a map, a chair, and headed straight for the beach. The word "tourist" written across my forehead wasn't necessary. Everyone could tell.

As I was crossing Princess Kaiulani Boulevard I clearly heard an impression form into words in my consciousness: "You will meet the princess later in this life." What a shock! I then came to Queen Liliuokalani Boulevard. "Someday you will meet this queen, too." Another shock!

I felt an immediate connection with Hawaii. I loved the beaches, the flowers, the history, and the people. It was home; but my destiny lay elsewhere. Several years later, now back in Oregon, I was invited by friends to a party in the Columbia Gorge. A woman named Cybil, who had recently moved up from California, was the owner of the house near Hood River. Her relatives were visiting from Vancouver, BC, Canada.

The host's mother and I hit it off immediately. While we talked, the memories slowly began to return, fragments at first, but I knew without a doubt that Cybil's mother had been the Queen in times past. Cybil's sister came to Oregon at a later date. There was an immediate air of familiarity. The prophecy I'd been given when I was twenty-eight crossing Princess Kaiulani Boulevard had been fulfilled. To my knowledge, I've never met the king.

Meeting friends from my past carried fond memories, but they were tempered with sadness. We'd been together on the islands when the queen had been tricked into forfeiting Hawaii to the dark forces. Even though we'd all moved on, it was evident that the wounds had not fully healed.

The Root Cellar

Another life-changing experience happened at a Waikiki bookstore. On three separate occasions, earlier in the month, I had awakened remembering a peculiar dream. I was digging a square pit somewhere beside a lake in a wooded area. The ground was hard, so the going was slow and laborious. At one point I became very frustrated as my shovel hit thick tree roots. I gave the dreams little attention, because they seemed to have no bearing at all on my current circumstances.

Then a book practically jumped off the shelf in the bookstore. It was an anthology of an early American writer's work. Almost immediately I turned to a page describing this author's misfortune while digging the root cellar for his cabin. While reading an essay, the rhythm of the sentences struck me as familiar. What little writing I'd done so far in this life could have passed for the author's.

Years later I had the opportunity to travel back to the east coast and walk the property that I'd read about in the book. Without going into detail, I was shown that the author's life had not ended in failure as he'd died believing. Most of his work had gone unpublished while he was living. Now, even his notebooks had been printed and distributed.

Selected writings had been translated into several languages. Gandhi successfully used principles of peaceful noncompliance found in one essay to liberate India from the British. It was very gratifying to return to the site of the reconstructed cabin, but not in an egotistical sense. I felt the universe smiling with me that day.

When I first heard about reincarnation, I knew from past experience that it was valid. We've all been famous at some point, just as we've all been infamous and obscure. We've struggled as drug addicts more often than we've been celebrated as saints. Bolstering the ego does no good. Sometimes we're given glimpses of our past in order to better understand our present lifetime. Past and future are only relevant from our human perspective. In actuality, the past, present, and future exist simultaneously.

The Simple Heart

While in the fifth grade I was given a clear glimpse of a past incarnation. Originally I wrote about it in the third person. It's hard to explain, but to memorialize it otherwise would be like drinking vintage wine from a paper cup.

As the story goes, a fifth grade teacher asked her students to bring a bar of soap to school on a certain day. The children exchanged puzzled looks, but the woman offered no explanation. When the day arrived, the teacher passed out carving knives and asked each student to carve something special from their bar of soap.

One boy was totally absorbed in his work. An hour flew by. At last he put down his knife and glanced about the room. He was surprised to find that he was the last one to finish. Some of his friends had carved lifelike animals; some had carved detailed faces; other's, miniature toys. The boy lowered his head, feeling very embarrassed, for he had chosen only a simple heart.

But as he looked down at the heart, a door to his past opened up before him. The boy found himself gazing out upon a time in history when renowned artists were producing lasting works of art. He was shown beautiful and intricate sculptures, carved from stone by his own hands. Many still stood, though centuries had passed, and were cherished by people from every land.

As quickly as the door had opened, it closed. Once again the boy stared down at the simple heart feeling very ashamed. He realized that his hands still held the gift; he could have chosen any number of difficult subjects like those of his classmates. Tears swelled in his eyes.

Above the boy's left shoulder an angel appeared. Very compassionately the angel bent down and whispered something in the boy's left ear, something the boy would never forget. He said, "There is nothing more pleasing to the eyes of God than the beauty of a simple heart!"

*   *   *

"His greatest work of art was now complete,
but the masterpiece had not been the image once
bound in stone. It had been the image of perfection
struggling to free itself from his own heart."

—Michael Harrington,
*Porcupines at the
Dance*[5]

−3−

Signs and Synchronicity

In the spring of 2001 I was just finishing the first draft of *Dragon's Breath*. In fact, I had it with me in the car. Meeting the Chief today at Colliding Rivers was very synchronistic, since many of our conversations were recorded in the book. In subsequent springs, beginning in 2005, I would return to Colliding Rivers to donate a few books to the Colliding Rivers Information Center and remember this day.

Had I looked for signs and synchronicities, I probably would have found them in abundance. They would likely have prepared me somewhat for the afternoon ahead. But I was lost in my inner world of thought and reverie. Roseburg was a little over an hour away now. From there, Highway 138, the road leading up to Crater Lake, would drop me off at Colliding Rivers in about twenty-five minutes.

One landmark travelers notice while passing by Roseburg on Interstate 5 is the Veteran's Administration Hospital adjacent to the freeway. Ken Kesey, the author, worked there at one time, as had I, in my early twenties. Some of the residents at the hospital had inspired the characters in Kesey's movie, "One Flew Over the Cuckoo's Nest."

A friend and I applied for summer jobs at the "VA," and were both hired on as Nursing Assistants. Jamie's dad was a nurse on one of the locked units. Even from the guarded entrances to those wards you could feel the dark, intense psychic energy pulling at you. Fortunately, I was stationed in a far less stressful section. I learned quickly, however, that the medical field wasn't for me. But for three months I gave it my best shot . . . well, sort of.

My experience with one of the residents taught me how the universe is intricately connected. I can attest to the fact that karma does exist, even if years pass before an action is balanced.

Pike's Peak Karma

Raleigh was a grizzly, ill-tempered old man who happened to be blind. No one on Ward 3 liked attending to him, and many were downright afraid. As the newcomer on the block, Raleigh was passed off on me with one piece of advice: Don't mention Pike's Peak! It made him crazy for some reason. Of course I wouldn't do anything that insensitive, I assured my coworkers.

One day, however, a mischievous mood came over me as I was leading Raleigh into the rest room. He was holding onto one of my arms, rather tightly I might add, when I blurted out, "Aren't you the one who took a leak at Pike's Peak?" Raleigh went wild. He flew into an indiscernible rant and violently scratched my arm with his fingernails. Apparently the advice about Raleigh had been correct.

Several years later the summer job at the VA Hospital was but a distant memory. After leaving a slightly less dismal job in Denver, I struck out on a sightseeing tour of southeastern Colorado. My aging sports car had recently been tuned up and, with my newfound freedom, I was on top of the world.

The views from my windows were breathtaking. Meadows of wildflowers passed by on the left; a tall, snow-capped mountain towered above me on my right. But then I noticed steam boiling up over my hood. The temperature gauge was pegged. Panicked, I pulled over and stopped. Ten minutes later the car finally cooled down enough for me to remove the radiator cap. Fortunately I carried a gallon jug of water with me for just such emergencies. As I was refilling the radiator some water splashed down on the ground. That's when I heard it: "Aren't you the one who took a leak at Pike's Peak?" The mountain I had been enjoying before my unexpected pit stop had been Pike's Peak! I burst out laughing.

Isn't it amazing how the Law of Cause and Effect crosses boundaries of time and space. Years may pass before our thoughts and actions are called in for balancing. It's no wonder some people complain of bad luck. When we create "outside of love," our creations must one day be brought back into balance.

Apology to the Frogs

When I was working at the smoky plywood mill in Sutherlin, I did my share of complaining. I was grateful for the job, however. When I was in my twenties the mill gave me refuge on numerous occasions. My favorite job was glue mixer.

One day my supervisor brought in boxes and boxes of rubber gloves covered with dried glue. He politely asked me to wash them in my spare time. Why were we washing the layup line's gloves? I wondered. Couldn't we just buy new ones like we'd always done, I grumbled to myself? My "spare time," when the batch of glue was mixing, was reserved for reading.

Washing gloves was not something I wanted to do, but I didn't argue. There must be a reason for such foolishness, I reasoned. And there was. It took me several months and hundreds of washed gloves to figure it out. As I was watching the latest load of gloves bob up and down in the rickety open-top washer, it struck me. The gloves looked like frogs trying to get out of the machine!

My task had not really been about washing gloves; it had been about cleansing my past actions. Some friends and I had killed frogs when we'd been younger. Their legs were a delicacy. In doing so, I had incurred a debt to life that was now being called in for balancing. I took responsibility for my destructive actions, and apologized profusely to the frogs for taking their lives for my own gratification. I had already stopped hunting several years earlier.

A few days later my supervisor strolled into my work area smiling broadly. "No more washing gloves," he announced. "We're going back to buying new ones. The layup crew complained that the washed ones were too slippery." And that was that. I went back to my reading.

Mixing glue was toxic, yet easy work. The poisons were a nice compliment to the mercury I'd already picked up in my youth. They played prominent roles in a dangerous health drama later in life. I won't go into it here, but there was a silver lining. One great line came out of the experience: "Sometimes God gives us our greatest gift disguised as our worst nightmare!"

One chilly morning my glue tanks were brimming, so I decided to catch up on some reading. My working area was located about ten feet off the ground. Heating coils fastened below the support grating were a welcome touch. Spillage from bags of flour and crushed walnut shells would fall through the grate to the concrete floor below. Clean up was easy. I simply hosed it down occasionally.

The glue loft was isolated from the rest of the mill, so I was rarely interrupted. The door directly across from me, which led outside to the tanks, was propped open that day. There was no breeze, and no one else was around. Without warning, the door suddenly slammed shut with such force that dust fell from the rafters. A powerful impression reverberated through my consciousness: "A door to your past is closing!"

Almost immediately a long-term relationship ended. A week later the mill closed down due to rising veneer costs. A careless driver then sideswiped my car. The changes hit me hard. But when a door closes, another one opens. I was ready to move on, and the universe knew it.

Interpreting Waking Dreams

In a wooded area not far from Colliding Rivers a small fir was growing from the surface of an old stump. I'd spotted it during an autumn outing and decided to return with a camera one Saturday in mid-December. To my disappointment, someone had chopped down the tiny tree since my previous visit.

Unusual events like this are sure indications that life is communicating in its symbolic language, the language of waking dreams. Carl Jung, the psychologist, called these events "meaningful coincidences."[1] I'd noticed my first one when I was eight. Ironically, that first one was the most powerful waking dream of all. I've never revealed it because it prophesied something that has yet to materialize.

The odds of someone hiking into that remote meadow and chopping down the very tree I'd singled out for my photo were extremely remote. That qualified it as a "message" from Divine Spirit, my Higher Self, or perhaps a Guardian or Master.

To decipher messages of this nature only requires a little awareness. Generally one or two questions will quickly find the link: "What was I thinking at that moment?" or, "What is the present focus of my life?" Waking dreams may also appear at the beginning of cycles, as well. These are more difficult to pin down.

After leaving the mill I was thinking of taking up art while I revamped my life. I'd planned to use the photo of the tree as a model for painting. I was being guided through this waking dream; a painter I would not be. Instead, I wrote a poem about the tiny tree and weathered stump. While the poem was no masterpiece of literature, it pointed me in the direction I was destined to pursue.[2]

Writers and speakers often find confirmations through waking dreams. After I'd written "Befriending Bigfoot" in Chapter One, for example, I flipped on the television and discovered a documentary entitled, "The Search for Bigfoot." Valuable "help" will come our way during the writing process if we only pay attention. I've had my computer mouse and keyboard suddenly freeze after writing something that didn't fit with my theme;

pages have mysteriously disappeared overnight after saving them before retiring; I've had unusual events occur regularly when focusing on specific topics.

For instance, while writing this section on waking dreams I decided to include some examples from a previous book. I was shown that a couple of my selections would be out of place. To monitor the water quality of the distribution system where I work, we have two different sampling routes. Each consists of fourteen sites. These specific locations never change. While sampling on Route Two recently, I noticed that two sites from Route One had mistakenly been included in my current route. No one at the lab knew how this mix-up had happened. It was a mystery to them. But I knew that the universe was speaking through this waking dream. Two items in my current project (this book) were out of place.

Warning messages hit the consciousness harder. Once I was walking through a rough neighborhood late at night. I'd stopped at a convenience store to purchase a cup of coffee moments before. As I walked along uneasily, I debated whether it was safe to keep going. At that moment a leaf fell from somewhere in the darkness above me and landed directly in my cup. Hot coffee spilled onto my hand and burned it. I turned around.

My friend, Jamie, told me about a waking dream he'd recently experienced, warning him about his health. Each day at work he made a routine visit to the pop machine down the hall in the building where he worked. The snack machine area was a popular destination for many of the building's occupants.

One day Jamie noticed a pattern. Whenever he would arrive at the pop machine, someone else would be there, too. Each time it would be a different person, but they all had one thing in common. They all had health problems or disabilities.

Jamie reached out to the universe, "If I'm being told that my health is taking a hit from drinking too much pop, then I'd like a definite confirmation. The next day he returned for his afternoon treat. This time he was alone. As Jamie made his selection, he breathed a sigh of relief. He reached down to get his drink, but to his surprise, there was nothing there. The machine had run out of cups and his pop had gone down the drain!

Synchronous Events

Unusual events may come in groups, generally in threes, which make them easier to detect. These are called "synchronous events." A pattern is repeated, so the observer takes notice. For example, a young woman may be considering a marriage proposal. Waking dreams could confirm that the match is a good one. She may even ask for guidance on the matter beforehand.

She could be driving to work and notice a license plate on the car ahead that reads, "Match." The positive guidance might show up again at work during a break when she overhears a coworker speaking about her new shoes and purse: "A perfect match!" Over lunch, a friend might casually mention a soup recipe she's found. The butternut squash and apple blend was "a match made in heaven."

A vocabulary of symbols begins to take shape automatically once we become aware of this secret language. For instance, a closing door might indicate that "a cycle is ending." Pike's Peak might represent either "inappropriate behavior," or "karma being balanced." Unlike in our nighttime dreams, we can consciously assign a value to any symbol and it will mean just that.

We can also use waking dreams to "bookmark" an event. For instance, we can ask for guidance on the proper time to move to a new location. When a certain symbol appears, we will know that it's time. One person picked "Aces and Eights," a poker hand, as his symbol. It was not so obscure that it could never come up; yet not so common that he would see it every day. Aces and eights are known as "the dead man's hand." When death symbols come up, they generally mean the end of a cycle, not termination of life.

When I developed a pain in my right side, I used a waking dream to advise me on a course of action. I didn't feel it would be necessary to select a specific symbol; I simply asked for an easily-interpreted sign that would warn me if the pain was something more than pulled muscles.

That entire morning I was more attentive than usual. For nearly three hours not a thing came up. I was about to pass the irritation off as a byproduct of moving a heavy chair a couple of days earlier, when a motorhome pulled up at an intersection on the country road I was traveling. It had brought with it my answer. The vehicle was a mobile medical lab. In large letters I read, "Any Lab Test Now." Without hesitation I made an appointment with my health care practitioner for that afternoon. The advice had been accurate. My appendix was inflamed.

Some waking dreams are easily deciphered, while others take more effort. Recently three separate incidents had me scratching my head. I sensed they were connected, but what did they mean? I could find no relationship with either my current thoughts or the present focus of my life.

Riddle of the Fox

The sequence began when I pulled up at a traffic light where a white pickup truck had stopped across from me. An animal had its head sticking out of the window. At first glance I thought it was a small dog. Upon closer examination, however, I discovered that it was a fox! How peculiar. Not something you see every day. I have a cat that loves to ride. People stare when they see him with his head out the window, too. But a fox?

A day later the second symbol appeared. I'd gone for a short walk along a familiar tree-lined path. Directly before me, about eye level, I spied a large leaf that had become entangled in a spider's web. The trees on either side of the path were at least fifteen feet away.

After puzzling over the two strange events, I forgot about them for a few days. My nephew was playing in a football game in Sutherlin. As I passed by the practice field I was greeted by another mysterious sight— hundreds and hundreds of tents. All told, there were approximately two thousand tents spread out across this field and an adjacent one. A lady at the concession stand filled me in. Sutherlin High School was the staging area for "Bike Oregon." Riders from all over the country would be assembling here in a few days.

Brainstorming on the image of a fox, I came up with "sly," "clever," "crafty." The leaf suspended in the web was either "caught" or "supported." It took a friend to shed light on the city of tents. She repeated slowly, thinking out loud, "the bikers were staying in tents— "intense!"

Putting the pieces together, I speculated that I was headed for an intense encounter with someone who would appear helpful, but would turn out to be sneaky, or manipulative. A relationship would develop that would hinder my progress.

When I revealed my conclusion to a new friend, one who had recently come into my life, she suggested that I use a more positive approach to interpretation. She suggested that a fox could also mean lucky. I couldn't think of an alternative to intense, but the leaf could very well have been supported, rather than caught. It was good advice, but lucky and supportive didn't fit with my current vocabulary of symbols. Of course I could change the meaning of fox from crafty to lucky, and webs from caught to supportive. Future waking dreams would reflect this change.

Hindsight often is the final determinant. My interpretation turned out to be wrong. Intense was correct. The leaf had indeed been supported; but the fox turned out to represent Jake, my cat. He developed a challenging health problem that required extensive support. A waking dream guided me to an unexpected source for help.

After doing laundry, I discovered that one of my pillowcases was missing. I distinctly remembered tossing both in the washer, but now one was gone. Usually my dryer ate socks. Finally I discovered the pillowcase behind the dryer. Okay, there is "one missing," I thought. But what?

Later that day I visited a friend who happened to be a nutritionist. She had offered some valuable suggestions three years earlier when I'd been detoxing from mercury and chemicals. She had also pinpointed specific foods that my body resonated with through a form of muscle testing. When I mentioned my cat's problem, she asked,

"Well, why didn't you bring him with you?" My cat was the missing one.

I took Jake by to see her the following day. Not only did we solve his immediate problem, but Jake received additional help that greatly improved his life.

The Three White Eagles

We can select specific symbols to represent milestones in our lives. When a particular symbol appears, it provides verification that we have reached that step. Sometimes symbols become part of our waking dream vocabularies without our conscious awareness. A synchronicity involving three white eagles confirmed a spiritual initiation.[3] A trip to San Francisco started it off.

A girlfriend had asked me to ride down to California with her to visit family who had recently relocated there. Sheila's mom knew that I was interested in books on philosophy and metaphysics. She had saved a copy of one she thought I might enjoy. The book featured the sayings of White Eagle, a Native American.

The following night we met Sheila's brother across town at one of his friend's house. It was the most miserable, rainy night you can imagine. Since Sheila was reluctant to drive in a strange city on a rainy night, I offered to drive her brand new Nissan 300 ZX. I was a little ill at ease on the drive over as I traversed unfamiliar territory in rush hour traffic, but not nearly as uncomfortable as on the way back.

Sheila's brother wanted to test-drive her new car, so he suggested a trade. It was fine with her, as long as I agreed to drive his recently purchased forty thousand dollar limousine. We were to follow him across town. What an exciting offer!

He lost us immediately. We didn't see him again on the flooded roadway. Trucks screamed by, flinging rooster-tails of water upon the windshield in greater amounts than the wipers could clear. Road construction signs appeared in the road only yards ahead, causing me to swerve to avoid them. Lanes disappeared suddenly without warning.

My nerves were on overload as I crossed bridges towering hundreds of feet above seething bays. As I approached the Golden Gate Bridge I received an impression from within: "This has been an outward reflection of an inward test." At last we pulled off on a quiet side street leading up to Sheila's mother's house. I breathed a sigh of relief as I locked the door and walked behind the back of the limo. The car's TV antenna, located in the center of the trunk, caught my attention. It reminded me of a bird with outstretched wings, a white eagle.

The highlight of the weekend was an impulsive, late night skiing trip to Lake Tahoe. We arrived early in the morning, ate a quick breakfast, and hit the famous slopes. Despite the crowds, we managed to get in a few good runs, which made the trip worthwhile.

On Monday we left San Francisco for home. Sheila drove as I slept; but near the Oregon border I awoke with a start. We were just clearing a heavy embankment of fog when I sat upright. Suddenly, a huge white bird veered in front of our windshield, then disappeared into the fog we had just passed through.

"What was that?" Sheila asked excitedly.

"An eagle," I answered calmly. "A giant white eagle."

It wasn't long after the California trip that I began to seriously consider writing a book about waking dreams. Since I'd never recorded a single one, I anticipated a long and difficult struggle. Instead, the book practically wrote itself. Several contributions from the schoolmate I mentioned earlier, Jamie Davis, helped fill in some gaps.

In reviewing the variety of waking dreams from my own life, I was struck by their practical nature. There'd been insights, guidance, and confirmations on many decisions that I'd made. Some had been important; others had been rather trifling. Waking dreams had both informed and warned me.

I was fascinated to discover that others had reported similar benefits. This included several historical personalities. For example, while doing research, I learned that Napoleon had been adept at recognizing waking dreams. But on two occasions they had brought him unsettling news.

Napoleon's Presentiments

Napoleon was a firm believer in prophetic events. For instance, one day word reached him from Egypt that one of his Nile boats, *L'Italie*, had run ashore and its French crew had been executed. Napoleon was very concerned. He saw this as an omen that his plan to annex Italy to France would fail. "My presentiments never deceive me," he said, "and all is ruined. I am satisfied that my conquest is lost." And he was right.[4]

It is reported that waking dreams also revealed something about Napoleon's wife's behavior. One day, without provocation, Josephine's picture fell over and the frame was cracked. Napoleon responded, "Either my wife is very ill, or she is unfaithful." It was the latter.[5]

I can relate to Napoleon's betrayal by his wife. An old girlfriend loved the moon, especially the crescent moon. That became her symbol in my vocabulary of waking dreams. Cindy lived about three hours away. Sometimes I would gaze up at the moon, knowing that it was shining down upon both of us at that very moment. There was often a single star tucked snugly in the crescent. I felt loved and secure.

One weekend Cindy told me she'd been shopping for shoes with a coworker in Eugene, about an hour away. Waking dreams told me otherwise! After talking with her on the phone about her trip, I noticed that my tee shirt was turned inside out. This was out of the ordinary, but no cause for alarm.

Minutes later I drove to the nearby coffee shop to buy a card for a friend. To my surprise, the first card I came across featured a crescent moon. In the crescent were two stars! My heart sank. Like Napoleon, I knew that the one I loved had been unfaithful.

Waking dreams have guided and fascinated me since I was young. Had I kept a journal, who knows how many I could have chronicled? The most important ones stuck in my memory, however. In 1990 *The Secret Language of Waking Dreams* was accepted by a small Midwest publisher. Two doors suddenly opened. One led to my greatest joy, that of becoming a published author. The other led to my darkest fear.

*   *   *

"Synchronicity is an ever present reality
for those who have eyes to see."
—Carl Jung, 1875–1961
Founder of Analytical
Psychology[6]

–4–

Sedona

In *The Secret Language* I mention in passing that my favorite waking dreams are those whose meaning keeps eluding me. They put magic in my life and give it an aura of excitement. My most memorable, unsolved, waking dream was one in which a white bird flew across the constellation of the Big Dipper one cold winter night. In retrospect, I can now say with confidence that this waking dream was confirming that I'd crossed a threshold. White birds have come to represent "initiations" in my working vocabulary.

Initiations boost an individual's vibrations and lead to greater self- awareness. In the weeks or months prior, excess baggage, stuff not needed for the next leg of the journey, is cleaned out and discarded. It's like moving to a new house in a way. In their truest sense, initiations bring a person closer in line with their true, spiritual self within. Furthermore, initiations can also link an individual with the Audible Life Stream, the great spiritual current flowing out of and returning to the highest heavens.

Fall Creek

A little after twelve-thirty I turned off Interstate 5 at Roseburg and drove south on Stevens Street toward the Diamond Lake turnoff. My meeting with the Chief at Colliding Rivers was scheduled for two-thirty. Many years before, just days after returning from California with Sheila, I'd been asked a question on this very same road. I'd been on my way to eat lunch at Abby's Pizza at the time.

It had come from out of the blue: "Would you like to go further?" Even though I had never dealt with this particular master, I recognized his vibration immediately. He was asking if I was interested in going further into the spiritual worlds on my journey of Awakening.

Despite the shock, I managed to answer offhandedly, "Yes, I'd like to go further."

"Very well," came the response, "if you're serious, then meet me at the bench along Fall Creek by nightfall."

It was not a physical voice, but an impression. It was accompanied by a short, approving nod. Had I heard correctly, or had it simply been my imagination? To be safe, I resolved to leave town immediately and make the one-hour drive to Fall Creek. Another half hour's trek would get me to the bench near the waterfall well before dusk. The one-mile, round trip hike to the falls was one of my favorites.

The secretary at the real estate office where I worked called. I was needed across town right away to meet with a potential renter. Not what I wanted to hear. I'd have to skip lunch. And then two more time-consuming "emergencies" came up. It was getting late. There was still ample time to make the drive, but I

48

was a little nervous as I left Roseburg. The traffic was heavier than usual, even though rush hour had been over for nearly forty-five minutes. I glanced down at my gas gauge. It was almost on empty.

By the time I finally pulled into the parking lot at the base of the Fall Creek trail, the sun was setting. I reached for my flashlight, the one I always kept with me in the glove box. To my dismay, it was gone! Common sense and a healthy dose of self-doubt told me to go back home. But curiosity and determination urged me forward. At worst, I thought to myself, I'd get lost in the darkness and have to spend the night on the trail; but there was also the possibility that something magical might happen. So, I stumbled onward through the last light of day toward a potential meeting with destiny.

A deer jumped out from a thicket beside me, scattering loose rock with its hooves as it bounded up the trail ahead. How different the woods appear at night. My heart began to pound heavily. In the dying light of day I could just make out the bench about twenty yards ahead. No one was there. I was relieved, but also a little disappointed. As a symbolic gesture, I bent down and touched the arm of the bench with a forefinger. I wheeled about without stopping to rest, wondering how I would make it safely to the bottom with a new moon as my only guide.

As I felt my way down the trail I heard the adept's words reverberating through my consciousness: "Very well," he said matter-of-factly, "the easy part's over."

The easy part's over? I repeated the words slowly, trying to make my brain understand what I had just heard. The easy part's over. Not a pleasant thought considering what I'd gone through already. I won't go into it here, but the list was substantial. [Most, if not all, of the hardships we encounter on the road to Awakening are of our own creation. They have arisen from the past when we've "created unconsciously" without love. The Chief believed that by cleaning out the Seedbed, or polishing the Mirror of God, we could transcend our limitations rather quickly. In *Dragon's Breath* he revealed his Golden Formula, one method of accomplishing this.[1]] I heaved a sigh of relief when I finally found my way to the parking lot in the inky blackness. So far, so good.

On the bright side, I thought, how bad could it be? (Cartoon images should come up here.) And, I was stronger for what I'd been through thus far. Death didn't even concern me that much. I tried to reassure myself that I'd made the right decision. For the most part, I was feeling fairly positive about my future on the drive back to town . . . but I'd completely forgotten about door number two.

Door Number Two

Behind door number two was my greatest fear— public speaking. That door had opened the day my waking dream book had been accepted for publication. The universe knew that I'd never volunteer to tackle this fear on my own, so it trapped me with my own success.

This was no ordinary fear. It was the mother of all fears, intricately linked with death. That's what gave it the teeth. Painful images from the past bubbled up during the healing process. More than once I'd been killed for speaking the truth. To be honest, my fear bordered on terror. My goal in life was first and foremost to avoid it at all costs; then, when all avenues to the higher worlds had been blocked, face it as courageously as I could.

Speaking before a group of any size was well beyond my comfort zone. I had avoided a confrontation with this fear for half a lifetime. Then, one morning I woke up and decided that the time had finally come. It was as simple as that. I was determined to overcome it or die trying. Once I'd made up my mind, the universe flew into action.

At a bookstore in Eugene I happened to run into Jim Stout, the organizer of a small seminar scheduled for the following Sunday, exactly one week away. He remembered a story I had recently told him, and offered to let me have five minutes on his program. He knew of my fear, and later observed that I'd looked like someone about to be thrown off a cliff. My hands were clammy, my face was ashen, and my body was shaking; so it was a total shock to hear myself say, "Yes." As I drove home from Eugene I asked the universe for help. A more desperate plea I can't imagine. And help came.

I began to make notes and, to my surprise, soon had a whole page full. A wind whistled through an open window and blew my notebook shut. Each time I reopened it, the wind would blow it shut. It was clear what I was being told. I would receive help with my talk, but I couldn't rely on notes. [I did, however, carry a card inside my back pocket. I wasn't ready to work without a net, and the universe allowed me that concession.]

I had a problem. The talk that came through was more than five minutes. In a mixed state of panic and boldness I called Jim Stout. "Ten minutes," I demanded. "Give me ten minutes."

By Tuesday night I was a nervous wreck. Three alternatives came to mind: leave town, step in front of a truck, or give the talk. The latter was the least appealing. Things began to change on Wednesday. I awoke in the middle of the night gazing into the bright blue eyes of a spiritual teacher. As his image faded, I realized that he'd been working with me in the dream state. Since my plea for help had been so passionate, I garnered the attention of other teachers.

On one occasion I was asked a question: "What was your attitude when you were learning to play baseball?" I remembered that I had experienced no fear, only determination to succeed. I knew that I was better than most of the others because I had practiced longer and harder. If I were to approach public speaking with the same attitude, I realized that I couldn't fail.

I soon discovered that by constantly editing my thoughts I could keep images of failure to a minimum. Imagination was another key. "Thinking from the end is the utmost, ultimate secret." Recently I'd heard that line someplace, and began repeating it over and over each day. I imagined people coming up to me after the seminar and complimenting me on my talk. I saw Jim Stout walk up to me afterwards and shake my hand.

On Thursday I practiced my ten-minute talk a dozen times. Whenever a thought of failure would crop up, I'd pull it out like a weed. I wasn't allowed to start off by saying, "This is my first talk and I'm pretty nervous." That would be admitting failure from the start. These kinds of barbs could puncture my balloon. From the onset, I would have to play the part of an experienced, confident speaker.

I was led to a conference room in a nearby motel that had been left unlocked by accident. For two hours on Friday I stood behind the podium, speaking into a microphone for the first time. I began to feel a little less intimidated while standing at the front of a room.

One self-help book told about a technique for handling pressure. It said to picture a ringing telephone in your mind. This could represent the panic signal going off on the way to the talk, for example. In the technique, you purposely ignored the telephone, telling yourself that you would answer it tomorrow. I decided that I would not think about success or failure until the day following the talk. I would just give it in a detached, indifferent manner and worry about results later.

When I adopted this attitude I stumbled upon something else. When I focused entirely on the talk, it gave the illusion that my life ended at that point in time. It was a form of death, so to speak. I found that by focusing on what I would be doing after the talk—like driving home with friends, celebrating my success, and planning a vacation—the energy wouldn't build up so much around that one event. I found that I was more relaxed in my preparation.

I made another important discovery. The more positive and confident I could become when practicing my talk, the better it seemed to flow. There was an invisible line I would cross if I became very determined and could eliminate thoughts of how the audience was reacting to my words. There was an outflow of energy instead of an inflow.

On Saturday night I lay in bed reviewing the week. It had lasted forever. I hadn't accomplished a thing at work. I'd spent every minute in preparation for the talk. It would all be over tomorrow by noon.

When I awoke at five-thirty a strange peace pervaded my consciousness. It was a three-hour drive to Wilsonville, the site of the talk. Two hours into the drive I received an inner impression: "You know where you are, don't you?" I was asked. I didn't recognize the questioner, but I managed to answer that I believed I was still about an hour away. The answer had an air of kindness and compassion about it: "Soul Plane." Ah, that explained the feeling of calm and contentment. This was the gift I was given for taking on the challenge of a lifetime. It was the ultimate help, an act of grace. I was allowed to experience the peace of the fifth dimension that entire morning.

About a hundred people gathered to hear the seven speakers on the program. I was the first to be introduced. I was thankful Jim Stout didn't say, "Please welcome a first-time speaker . . ." There's no telling what that barb would have done to my concentration.

Very confidently I climbed the steps and took my place behind the podium. I noticed that my mouth was dry. Everyone stared up at the leadoff speaker expectantly. Ten minutes passed as I gave my talk for the thirtieth time—only this time it counted!

I said "thank you," then returned to my seat in the front row. My relief was so great that I had difficulty concentrating on the other speakers. I had done it. I'd just taken the biggest step of my life. By asking for help, controlling my mind, and using my imagination, I had overcome my biggest fear.

After the seminar a number of people approached me and said how much they had enjoyed my talk. One person confided that a "golden key" had floated through the air to him as I'd spoken. Another smiled and nodded.

A man knelt down beside my chair with his hand extended, smiling broadly. It was Jim Stout.

The Happiest Place on Earth

A month later I returned from a brief vacation in Hawaii. Now that I had given a talk and had faced my fear, I was looking forward to returning to my moderately stress-free life. The phone rang, interrupting my thoughts. It was someone calling to ask if I'd received the information on the talk I was to give at the upcoming metaphysical seminar in Anaheim.

"There must be some mistake," I stammered.

"No," the voice responded with a hint of suppressed laughter. "We'd like for you to give a fifteen minute talk on Sunday, April 3rd."

After an extended silence I answered him. "Why not?" I knew that it would be no more difficult than the one I had just given. And so, four months after my first talk, I found myself on my way to speak about waking dreams in front of several thousand people at a major metaphysical seminar.

A time change happened to fall on that particular weekend. Spring ahead—fall back. I knew the saying by heart, but still it threw me. I showed up at the airport exactly one week early! I know I shouldn't feel bad. It's probably happened to a lot of people.

I missed most of the seminar. I spent every waking moment controlling my imagination, editing my thoughts. Although I didn't realize it at the time, this process of choosing positive images marked the beginning of a huge breakthrough. It was the first step in consciously creating my own universe.

Saturday afternoon I went for a short walk and found myself at the gates of Disneyland. I gazed up at the famous sign, "The Happiest Place on Earth." I couldn't remember the last time I'd truly been happy.

Sunday morning the Anaheim Convention Center was packed. I stepped up my attitude. Going to the plate with a bat doesn't make you a hitter, I told myself. I summoned up every ounce of positive strength as I made the lonely walk to the back stage area. As I pulled the admittance pass from my wallet, something fell out on the floor. It was an old fortune from a fortune cookie. Not wanting to break my concentration, I tucked it away in my jacket pocket.

My talk was over before I knew it. The audience seemed to enjoy it. I went directly to my room and flopped down on the bed, just as I'd planned. I'd left the television on to give the room a welcoming air. Then I remembered the fortune. A warm wave of love surged through me as I read it aloud: "Everything will now come your way."

On the Road to Sedona

In 1985 two friends and I packed up a motorhome and set off for Arizona. Located in the heart of red rock country was a vortex of energy we'd heard about through word of mouth. This powerful vortex passed through the living room of a house situated on the Wings of the Wind Ranch a few miles outside of town.[2] The trip changed all three of us.

The first of three unusual incidents happened at a coffee shop in northern California. While Gary and I looked over the menu, Randy idly spun a quarter on the table in front of us. He held the coin on edge, then flipped the side to make it spin. For some reason, the spinning coin stuck in my mind.

As we passed through a desolate valley in Nevada, the "spinning" symbol appeared again. An impressive row of windmills lined the ridges surrounding us. From their lofty position, they appeared to be guarding the valley below. White blades spun in the sunlight. We drove on, puzzling over the hidden meaning of the spinning images, awaiting our next clue.

Near the border of Arizona I glanced up and saw something I have never forgotten. It was a flock of white geese, perhaps numbering a hundred, tumbling in a peculiar spherical pattern. Geese normally fly in the form of a V, but these were performing graceful aerial acrobatics.

I had recently read that a vortex produces sound-and-light energy as it spins. It also steps down current from a higher frequency. This principle had been demonstrated for us through waking dreams on our trip to Sedona. The fact that the birds in the aerial play had been geese revealed the genius of the Director. Geese had long been my symbol for the Inner Sound.[3]

Wings of the Wind

By a stroke of luck, or a smile from Divine Providence, we managed to find the Wings of the Wind property in Sedona. We had no map, the roads were poorly marked, and there were no identifying signs. But we drove right to it! I had always imagined the royal and cordial welcome we would receive by the caretaker of the estate. An elderly gentleman would amble over, accompanied by his aging Poodle, and greet us at the gate with a broad smile. "Welcome. Welcome," he would say.

"Please come up to the house for a cup of tea." This did not happen.

The current caretaker, Robert, did meet us at the gate. But his stride was not that of an elderly man. We subsequently learned of his martial arts background. Robert had finished his ninja training in Japan prior to taking the caretaking job at the ranch. Some of his ninja friends would "pop in on him" occasionally, he told us later.

Robert surveyed the three of us at length. Two Doberman Pinschers flanked him. They stood silent and still, scanning us intently. We saw no Poodles. One of the dogs had been struck in the eye by a rattler three days before, giving him an even more threatening look. A stately German Shepherd was part of the group, but chose to sit quietly about ten feet behind the welcoming party.

At last Robert invited us onto the property. Since the kitchen floor was being resurfaced, we wouldn't be allowed inside the house. But we could walk the property at our leisure, he told us. This was a huge disappointment.

I'd heard stories about the house. A vortex of energy poured down through the living room from its source in the God Plane. For many years I had dreamed of visiting this power point. Furthermore, I had also heard mention that drawings of masters lined the walls of the living room. To be standing only a few yards away and be denied the experience was crushing.

Robert listened politely as I told him how far we'd come and the reason for our visit. While I'd stated my case well, I got the feeling that it was not to be. Then, suddenly, Robert tilted his head toward the sky. Something was up. "Why don't you come on in," he offered graciously. "You can tour the house; just steer clear of the kitchen."

Robert continued. "Generally I keep to myself while people briefly tour the house, then I escort them out. But why don't you take your time. Please feel free to ask me anything you like." I was shocked. This was like handing a teenager the keys to a Corvette full of gas.

Gary, Randy, and I stepped gingerly into the living room. I wanted to drink it all in. This was better than Disneyland. I noticed the air. It was highly charged and vibrating intensely. Through the large picture window on the far side of the room we could see Cathedral Rock, the famous landmark, just beyond Oak Creek. It was larger than life. But looking through the vortex pulsing through the living room, the scene took on an ethereal quality. Cathedral Rock was swimming before our vision.

To me, it felt like the diameter of the spinning vortex extended about fifteen feet outward in all directions from the center of the room. For the next ten minutes or so, I thought to myself, I'll be standing in the spiritual current streaming down from the God Plane. Lining the walls were drawings of masters, some of whom I'd heard about; of others, I had not. Most were done in pencil, but a few had been drawn with colored pencil, too.

A drawing of Rama, the founder of a remote monastery in Tibet, caught my attention. He was depicted as a powerfully built man with wavy hair and piercing eyes. Although the drawing wasn't colored, the lightly tinted eyes depicted them as blue. How would anyone recognize a master from a pencil drawing, I wondered? (The drawing of Rama had prompted my question.) Without going into detail, I was shown later in the trip that these drawings were indeed fairly accurate.

Robert stepped into the room and offered to answer any questions we might have. Ten minutes turned into three hours! I am comfortable passing along a few things he told us. Much of his time was spent answering questions about his life. Robert talked about writing a book one day, but evidently never got around to it.

As I recall, while still a teenager, he studied with a shaman in the desert, much like Carlos Castaneda. In his twenties, Robert became a well-known Hollywood guru. He was on a first name basis with all the great teachers of the day, including Yogananda. Robert related that he could walk right out of his body in full consciousness. He would sleep only two or three hours a night. Devotees would comb his hair for him, fix his meals, and give him gifts, including cars. He laughed, extending his arms wide. "I had an ego this big," he admitted.

One day, during his guru era, Robert was in New York City near St. Patrick's Cathedral. A beggar approached him asking for money. Robert said he'd given him a hard time, telling him to get a job like everybody else. He'd walked less than a block when his inner teacher, whoever that was, sent him a message. "Ah, you blew it," he told Robert. "That was the master who was supposed to lead you to God in this lifetime." Robert wheeled about and ran back down the street, but the beggar had vanished. He did meet the adept who had tested him later, however.

Robert explained to us how he had been chosen for the caretaker job, and the remarkable way he'd been greeted. After moving his storable belongings into the barn, one of the masters popped in and asked Robert to accompany him outside. Robert continued his unpacking, stating that he was tired and wanted to finish so he could take a nap. But the adept was insistent.

Finally Robert gave in and followed him outside. Directly above him on the lawn hovered nine golden eagles. From their circular position overhead, they conveyed their personal greeting to the new caretaker of the Wings of the Wind.

[Note: Before releasing the above information I tried to contact Robert unsuccessfully. I decided to ask my "unseen editor" for permission through a waking dream. Confirmation would only come if I were to receive two symbols the following day: a golden eagle and the number nine. When I checked my email the next day I found a picture from a German artist named Eva, depicting a golden eagle. A second email came from a different source announcing a workshop called "The Nine Dimensions of the Heart."]

Cleaning the Wings of the Wind house every day was a top priority. The property was used by various masters to teach a small number of advanced students. To my surprise, Jalal al-Din Rumi, the famous Sufi, was one of the teachers Robert interacted with regularly. Robert confessed that it had taken him some time to warm up to Rumi, but eventually they had become friends. According to Robert, Rumi dresses well and wears a bright green turban.

Part of his cleaning duties involved sweeping the porches in the mornings. The job was not for the faint of heart. Because the vortex radiates such powerful positive energy, rattlesnakes congregate on the porches at night. When we finally exited the house, Robert warned us to watch our step.

Gary, Randy, and I each went our separate ways to survey the ranch. The view of Cathedral Rock was spectacular, but the desert landscape held little interest for me. Oak Creek was rumored to have healing properties. I'd heard stories of sick animals bathing in the waters and regaining their health. I tried to contemplate on a ridge overlooking the creek, but the sound of East Indian music coming from an adjacent property interrupted the silence and dampened the mood.

Over dinner the three of us reflected on the recent events, including the remarkable white geese that had so accurately depicted the spinning vortex. Gary was surprisingly quiet. We found out why. When he'd looked up, instead of seeing birds spinning as we had, he'd seen a regular flock of geese flying in a V-formation.

I then mentioned the music that had disturbed my contemplation. Randy asked, "What music?" Gary hadn't heard anything either, although they both had been walking in my vicinity. I realized that the music had come from my own inner worlds. The universe isn't cast in stone. Since we generally share common experiences, we tend to think it's the same for everyone. When we're ready to unravel the mystery, however, the universe will show us it's unique, holographic nature.

*   *   *

> "'Come to the edge,' he said.
> 'We are afraid,' they said.
> 'Come to the edge,' he said.
> They came. He pushed them
> . . . and they flew."
>
> —Guillaume Apollinaire,
> 1880–1918
> French poet, playwrite,
> novelist[4]

PART TWO

The Chief's Final Discourses

"The pain that you carry is the love you withhold, lifetime after lifetime."

—Morinea,
Alex Collier's
Andromedan Contact[1]

–5–

Invincibility of the Inner Warrior

A little after one o'clock the sign announcing the Colliding Rivers viewpoint came into sight. Since saying goodbye to the Chief and leaving the area in the fall of 1990, I had returned to Colliding Rivers a couple of times each year. The Umpqua River and its waterfall-rich tributaries had captured my heart as a kid. But after meeting with Mr. Redstone for close to three years at his cabin nearby, the area had taken on the feel of home. In an hour and a half I would see the Chief again, after a long hiatus. That made this trip even more special.

A black SUV was just pulling out of the Colliding Rivers parking lot as I shut off my engine. I was greeted by crisp river air and the swishing tail of a fleeting grey squirrel. Two engraved plaques were mounted on stands by the viewpoint wall. One described the methods early settlers had used in crossing the river. A second registered the high-water mark set by the 1964 flood. Tourists could survey the spectacle below from the solid rock wall. With the exception of rare storm events like "the big flood," however, the collision of Little River and the North Umpqua was less than earth-shaking. Today, high cumulus clouds gave the grounds a lackluster feel. It fit with my introspective mood.

Our trip to Sedona had set in motion many changes. For example, meeting Robert at the Wings of the Wind Ranch had inspired me to take up Tae Kwon Do. While I'd been more interested in exercise than in self-protection, I'd found the program's kicking techniques challenging and had stayed with it for nearly three years. Just prior to my black belt test, a fellow student brought in a story by Terry Dobson that affected me deeply. One of the Chief's last discourses came to mind when I heard it . . . but first the story.

Terry Dobson was a student of Aikido, a martial arts system based on benevolence and kindness. It was developed by Morihei Ueshiba, a Japanese "peaceful warrior," who died in 1969 at age eighty-six. When I imagine the elderly gentleman in Dobson's tale, I picture Mr. Ueshiba. Terry's life-changing incident took place on a train in a Tokyo suburb.[2]

Another Way

When Terry boarded the clanking old train it was nearly empty—only a few housewives with their children, some old folks out shopping, a couple of off-duty bartenders studying a racing form. Terry gazed absent-mindedly out the window at the dreary rows of houses lining dusty, crowded streets.

At one station the quiet was shattered by the bellowing of a drunken man. The large, slovenly-dressed laborer shouted violent and obscene curses as he boarded the train. His eyes were bloodshot, demonic.

His hair was crusted with filth. As the drunk staggered into the car, he swung his fist at the first person he saw, a woman holding a baby. The glancing blow sent her sprawling into the laps of an elderly couple.

The terrified couple jumped up and scurried away. The laborer kicked at the woman's back as she retreated, but missed. Enraged, he grabbed the metal pole in the center of the car and tried to wrench it from its base.

Terry was tough. He stood six feet in height and weighed 225 pounds. After practicing Aikido eight hours a day for over three years, he was ready for any challenge. Terry remembered the words of his teacher: "Whoever has the mind to fight has broken his connection with the universe." But in his heart, Terry had secretly hoped for an opportunity like this—to defend the weak from violent offenders like this one. People could get hurt, he told himself, if something isn't done fast.

Seeing Terry stand up, the drunk focused his rage on him. He would give this foreigner a lesson on Japanese manners. The drunk punched the metal pole with his fist to show he meant business, and gathered himself for a rush. A split second before he moved, someone shouted "Hey!" It was ear splitting. Terry remembered being struck by the lilting quality of the voice. It carried an undercurrent of joy. "Hey!"

Both Terry and the laborer wheeled about. An elderly Japanese man, well into his seventies, stared back at them. He paid little attention to Terry, but beamed delightedly at the laborer as though he had an important secret to share.

"C'mere," the old man called, beckoning to the drunk. "C'mere and talk with me." He motioned for the laborer to join him. The big man followed, as if on a tether. Planting himself belligerently in front of the elderly gentleman he roared, "Why the hell should I talk to you?"

The old man smiled sweetly, without fear or condemnation. "What'cha been drinking?" he asked lightly.

"I been drinkin' sake," the laborer bellowed back, splattering the old man with spittle. "And it's none of your goddam business!"

"Oh that's wonderful," the old man answered, "absolutely wonderful! You see, I love sake, too. Every night me and my wife, she's seventy-two, you know, we warm up a little bottle of sake and take it out into the garden, and we sit on the old wooden bench that my grandfather's first student made for him. We watch the sun go down, and we look to see how our persimmon tree is doing." He looked up at the drunk with twinkling eyes.

As he struggled to follow the intricacies of the old man's words, the drunk's face began to soften as his fists unclenched. "Yeah," he murmured slowly, "I love persimmons, too . . . " His voice trailed off.

"Yes, said the old man, smiling, "and I'm sure you have a wonderful wife."

"No, replied the laborer. "My wife died." He hung his head and began to sob. "I don't got no wife. I don't got no home. I don't got no job. I don't got no money. I don't got nowhere to go." His large body began to quiver, as tears streamed down his face.

Terry stood motionless, trying to absorb what had happened in front of him. His thoughts were interrupted as the train pulled up at Terry's stop. As he maneuvered toward the door, he heard the old man's compassionate words. "My, my," he clucked, "that is a difficult predicament, indeed. Sit down here and tell me about it."

As Terry exited the train he turned for one last look. The drunk's head was resting in the old man's lap. He saw the old man stroking the filthy, matted hair.

What Terry had wanted to do with resistance and force, the old man had done with a few kind words. Terry had just seen Aikido in action. Its essence was love. From that point forward, Terry practiced Aikido with a spirit of compassion.

Mt. Thielsen

The further we get from Source, the more separate and differentiated things appear to be. Viewing life with sleepy, third-dimensional eyes, it's easy to believe that we are separate from everything in our universe. But this is the illusion of our holographic reality. There is no separation, just as there are no enemies "out there."

In the spring of 1988, a few months before my brief move to Colorado, John Redstone and I drove up to Mt. Thielsen, an extinct volcano near Diamond Lake. I remember the chilly spring morning and the spectacular view from the 9,100-foot summit after our two-hour hike. Something the Chief had said that day stuck in my mind. He told me the word "paranoia" once had a different meaning. Rather than referring to an "unfounded fear" or delusion, he said that it had meant the "interconnectedness of all things." The meaning had been altered by those wanting to muddy the waters of truth with fear. Fear has been used to cut off our access to the wholeness of life. It has deadened our inner senses and kept us asleep.

The final thirty feet leading up to Thielsen's peak was steep. Loose shale made the footing even more treacherous. The Chief had climbed to the top on numerous occasions, but today he was content to wait below until I returned from the summit. We ate a light lunch of raisins, nuts, and seeds while enjoying the stunning view of Diamond Lake. Mr. Redstone began a discussion on "Wholeness." We had previously covered the light wave of creation, and how the Golden Thread connects every light wave in the universe.

Briefly, ideas are expressed from the Realm of Stillness, then voided back to stillness once their purpose has been fulfilled. This activity takes place in a cube-shaped vacuum chamber called a light wave. In the center of each light wave is a still point, the "fulcrum." Some call it the "zero point." This is the communication center of the light wave, where the Golden Thread connects each light wave with the heart of Oneness.

We are creators. Thinking is the process of dividing ideas into polar opposites in light waves. Once set in motion, we can experience these "reflections of reality" in our holographic universe. But we must also take responsibility for balancing all that we create outside of love.

Mr. Redstone continued his discourse on Wholeness on the slope of Mt. Thielsen.

JR (John Redstone): "Everything we come in contact with—the beautiful and the 'not so beautiful'—is only an extension of ourselves." The Chief's bright brown eyes twinkled. "Once we understand that Oneness has been reflected into multiplicity, we can begin to move toward reunification. Until we learn how the universe operates, we will complain, blame, judge, and deny. These keep us from waking up from the 'Dream of Separation.'

"When we sleepwalk through our world of dreams, we resist life, building boundaries rather than flowing with it and growing in understanding. Simply put, the more boundaries and resistance we put up, the more room there is for fear. The closer we get to acceptance and Unity Consciousness, the more space for love. Fear compresses and captures; love expands and liberates. So, how do we go about freeing ourselves from fear-based limitations like judgment and blame? And how do we go about opening ourselves to love?"

M: "Self-Responsibility?" I answered, knowing from our earlier conversations that this was correct, at least the initial step.

JR: "That's right. But did you know that responsibility includes every single thing in our lives?"

[I did. But I was still having difficulty grasping the "every" part.]

The Chief continued. "Oh, the chocolate-covered-cherry experiences are easy. We gladly take responsibility for these. But conflicts and disagreements with others, they're the real challenges. When we're having a problem with another person, there's one thing we can know for certain: we are responsible for attracting that situation. It's up to us to figure out why. So, 'understanding' must be the next key, right?"

[Over the years I have learned how the Chief would respond when people complained. One time, for instance, a woman mentioned that she was frustrated because a new neighbor had moved in who was rattling around late at night. He was very inconsiderate. "He's the perfect neighbor!" the Chief observed. "Isn't it remarkable how the universe arranged for him to move in right next door? He didn't move into the building down the street. He moved right into yours. What do you think he's reflecting for you? Perhaps there's something to be balanced?"

The Chief understood how the universe worked. This was reflected in his attitude and view of life. He tried to show each person with whom he interacted that being a victim hindered finding a solution. In the woman's case, he helped her change the way she viewed the noisy neighbor. The Chief suggested to the woman that she thank him inwardly for bringing her this experience. He was only the messenger. By blaming the other party, the issue could not be resolved. The Chief would often ask playfully, "How can we release a problem that is not ours?" He told the woman that if it were him, he would first take responsibility for attracting the experience, then use his imagination to put the problem into picture form. This bypassed the lower mind.

The Chief found that the solution would often present itself once he'd taken these first steps. Perhaps he'd been a noisy neighbor himself at one time, and this man was here to show him how that felt. By replacing blame with acceptance, love would do its magical work of balancing the energies. The noisy neighbor would suddenly decide to move, or else he would change his behavior.]

Continuing our discussion on Mt. Thielsen, I asked the Chief a question.

M: "What do you see as the biggest barrier to becoming whole?"

JR: "The big one is fear; but I'd say the most dangerous one is denial. Fear hits us right in the pit of the stomach. We can see it coming. But denial hides in the shadows and mocks us." The Chief then gave me an example I could relate to.

"For instance, we might encounter someone on a plane who demands preferential treatment. This arrogant individual might look back from his seat in first-class upon the 'common mortals' riding in coach with superiority. More likely, he would disregard them completely. Our first instinct is to judge this person harshly: Who does he think he is sitting up there on his high horse?" The Chief chuckled. "If we rush to judge this person, if he really gets under our skin, it's a sure indication that somewhere within us we have that very quality. If not, then he wouldn't bug us, or we would find ourselves on a different plane."

M: "Yes, I can relate," I answered. "I've felt that way on occasion." I told the Chief about a friend I'd worked with at the plywood mill who really took the cake. Shane was especially critical of professional athletes who changed teams for better contracts. Shane accused them of having no loyalty, of being totally self-centered and arrogant. These "prima donnas" really irritated him. He took fiendish delight in wishing them great misfortune. Shane was really reacting to his own arrogance and disloyalty hidden deeply within his Belief System. For him, and for most of the people I knew, this was a huge barrier in returning to Oneness. But was it an insurmountable one?

I confessed my own shortcomings in this area to the Chief. Remembering a line from "The Razor's Edge," the 1984 version of the movie starring Bill Murray, I added pensively, "It's easy to be a holy man on top of a mountain!"[3] [It was appropriate, considering our panoramic view from Mt. Thielsen.]

JR: Mr. Redstone glanced over knowingly. "Yes, it's easy to feel connected with all life here in the mountains."

M: I looked out toward the rim of Crater Lake and nodded. I suspected the reason being that no humans were around to push our buttons.

JR: "We are unconscious creators. We create outside of love, but don't want to face our creations. We deny, deny, deny. And this keeps a part of us disconnected. Furthermore, we would rather not face our less-than-admirable side, our shadow.

"The Mirror of Life brings us opportunities for Wholeness. When we see qualities mirrored in others that we don't like, we can recognize them as reflected parts of ourselves, parts we've denied. We can speak to these qualities, thank them for teaching us about our strengths and weaknesses, and welcome them back to love. This way they are balanced, or "zeroed out." Once we've done this, we will never have to deal with that particular reflection again. Our entire Seedbed will be transmuted to reflect our new understanding.

"When we see our own buried qualities reflected in other people, the ones that really bug us, we must avoid judging the person reflecting them. If we don't, we will be judging an aspect of ourselves we have pushed into denial. [Of course, we can evaluate their actions without judging them personally.] Keeping the lid on denial requires a great amount of energy.

"Acceptance is the opposite of denial. We must first take responsibility for having that quality within ourselves, and then welcome it back into loving acceptance." The Chief must have read my thoughts, for he smiled understandingly. "No, it's not easy to do this at first. But once we truly understand the process, we will look for opportunities to improve our lives. Think about it. There really aren't that many negative qualities in total. We can run through them fairly quickly once we understand the mechanics."

[To restate the founder of Aikido's words: "Whoever has a mind to fight has already broken his connection with the universe." The Chief, although not a student of martial arts, would likely have put it this way: "The warrior is greatest who never draws conflict to himself."]

On the mountain that day we talked more about reflection.

JR: "On numerous occasions we've discussed the Seedbed, the part of the mind that was split off from the higher mind to act as a repository of negativity. The contents of the Seedbed, or Belief System, are outpictured into physical reality on a daily basis. Our Higher Self brings only a small portion of it to our attention at one time. That way we don't end up in a heap. This baggage includes our denials, our limiting judgments, and our negative thoughts and actions waiting to be called in for balancing. Our fears are also rooted here."

[The Chief often pointed out how to recognize the next item to be balanced within our Seedbed. It is whatever is currently giving us physical discomfort, mental anguish, or emotional pain.]

JR: "People sometimes ask me about self-protection, how they can make themselves bullet proof, so to speak. Well, we do this by cleaning out the Seedbed. Two things come to mind here. First, a higher understanding will automatically transmute a belief or judgment of lower nature; and, secondly, emotions are magnetic.

"We constantly judge people as good or bad, pretty or ugly, happy or sad, and so forth. As we now know, we are really judging a reflection of ourselves, aspects we don't want to see. Judgment is not the best way to open the heart, but it does serve to divide and mislead." The Chief glanced over at me with a mischievous smile. "We judge ourselves harshly, too. How many times have we felt unworthy of love, inferior, ostracized, a failure? We truly have no idea how much we are loved. Our greatest lesson is learning to love ourselves the way God loves us. It begins with releasing judgments, and by catching ourselves when we criticize our reflections.

"I find that it helps to verbalize this process. As in the case of judgments, I generally say something like this: 'I release the judgment that I'm not worthy of love,' to pick an example. I follow up with a truth: 'I accept the truth that I am loved beyond measure.' This might bring up a bodily response. If there are trapped emotions and judgments to the contrary, we can search them out and release them."

M: "How did these emotions get trapped?"

JR: "Well, Michael, it may not have been acceptable to feel them at the time, or perhaps it was unsafe. In the case of anger, a person's religious peers might judge him as being unspiritual if he displayed anger. So he would keep this anger bottled up instead of feeling and releasing it. Or, expressing anger could have put him in danger. As a child, the person may have had an abusive father who would not tolerate anger being directed toward him in his own home. There are any number of instances where anger could have been stifled."

M: "Beneath anger we generally find fear," I interjected. I was speaking from experience.

JR: "That's right. And of course we deny some emotions because they're downright unpleasant to feel."

[I knew the Chief was on the mark. I'd experienced intense emotional trauma when my mom had died. I used alcohol to numb the pain. The emotions had been too overwhelming. Years later I'd had to feel the sadness and guilt, however. I'd just delayed the response. But I found out later, from the Chief in fact, that pain is multiplied when we deny or hold it.]

JR: "When we hold on to pain, it is filed away in the Seedbed in tight little packages that some have called "engrams." They carry powerful charges that cry out to be released. We magnetically draw experiences similar to the original one in an attempt to release the pain. If not successful, the stakes get raised. We will eventually attract an event into our life with enough emotional charge to release the pain we're holding."

M: "Can you give me an example?"

JR: "Sure, take fear. Say we are afraid of heights. The anxiety we get in the pit of our stomach when we cross bridges, for instance, will trigger this trapped fear. It could have originally been caused by falling from a cliff in another life. We will continue to get feelings of anxiety when we are looking down from high places until we get a charge large enough to match the original one, and then it releases if we allow it.

"The ancient Chinese knew this. They found that if they could get a person to bring up these trapped feelings, they could "pop" the engram by making a sudden loud noise. They would generally slam two bricks together. Today people pop balloons in some cases."

[I would later learn how love can accomplish the same thing. Because of its high vibration, it has the

77

ability to transmute all lower frequencies. Chapter Nine expands on this.]

JR: "Where trapped feelings reside, there will always be judgments surrounding them. It takes some sleuthing to uncover them at times. Take the case of anger again. A common judgment might be, "If I show anger I'll be punished," or, "If I show anger I'll be a bad person." How about this one? "If I get angry I'll go to Hell." After releasing the emotional charge and its accompanying judgment, remember to fill the void with a truth: 'I accept the truth that it's okay to feel and release emotions (anger) safely.'"

[I used a similar technique when facing my fear of speaking in public. Wrapped around the fear were several judgments: "If I speak the truth I'll be killed;" "If I speak the truth I'll be laughed at;" "If I speak the truth I'll be ostracized." Speaking in public is the number one fear. We've all taken big hits on this one. Fear of death is number two.

Our fear of speaking originates in the past. In one instance, I'd been hanged from a gallows in a public square for speaking my truth. Another time a friend had betrayed me in ancient Greece. I'd been a politician, giving a speech opposing the popular agenda, when a knife had been thrust into my gut. Both instances had resulted in my death, hence the powerful charge surrounding the judgments that were born from the traumas.]

JR: "Once we stop blaming and judging, even to a small degree, the 'High Road' begins to open up for us. The High Road leads to the heart. At this point in our journey we will likely be assaulted by fear. Fear is the enemy of the heart. Facing and releasing trapped fear is the biggest key to invincibility; it's the way to Oneness.

"There aren't too many different fears, so the task is not as daunting as it seems. Death wears many masks. By establishing self-knowledge about death we can clear the way quickly. Remember, a higher under-standing will automatically transmute all lesser truths or misconceptions.

"Wisdom and love both carry higher vibrations than the information stored in the Belief System. Either one may be used to transmute 'lesser truths.' Our entire Seedbed is then upgraded. Once we release an emo-tional charge, it will not be necessary to draw further experiences of that nature."

I'd brought up the subject of warriors earlier with the Chief. He alluded to this in closing our discussion.

JR: "There are those who spend a lot of time pre-paring for conflict. Unconsciously, these people fear their own denials. Resistance in any form will delay our return to Wholeness. There are no enemies 'out there.' But there are parts of ourselves waiting to be reclaimed from denial. There are judgments and fears crying to be released. They desperately want our love.

By cleaning out the Seedbed we open ourselves to love. It is also true that opening ourselves to love can assist in transmuting the Belief System. This makes us invincible. We will not attract harm or further hard-ship to ourselves."

M: I nodded approvingly.

JR: "If a person wants to be a warrior, then he or she should become a warrior of the heart, or a warrior of wisdom. Take responsibility for life; understand life; flow with life; surrender to life; fall in love with life.

79

This will lead to the *'Sat Shatoiya,'* the true reflection of the Divine."

*   *   *

"A true warrior is invincible
because he or she contests with nothing."
—Morihei Ueshiba,
1883–1969
Founder of Aikido[4]

–6–

The Dreamland Matrix

Rather than wait in my car for the Chief's arrival, I decided to take a short walk to the site of the old cabin. Not long after the Chief had moved to the Southwest, the rustic cabin had burnt to the ground. When news first reached me, it had felt like a part of my life had been lost, as well. So many of our discussions had taken place on the cozy back porch overlooking Little River.

The seven-acre parcel where the Chief had lived was the nearest privately owned property to Colliding Rivers. I secretly harbored dreams of buying it and resurrecting the cabin, with a few alterations. Perhaps I'd add a separate building dedicated to the memory of John Redstone and open it on weekends to the public. But, other than myself, who would appreciate the significance of a few old books and a handful of letters and photographs? Few of those living in Douglas County would see the difference between these treasures and your run-of-the-mill garage-sale stock.

As I neared the gravel driveway I noticed a white van backing out. Apparently the driver had missed a turn and was using the driveway as a turnaround. The nondescript van triggered a memory from earlier in the month. The universe had brought me yet another confirmation that life here is not what it seems.

The Unmarked Van

A coworker and I had stopped at a bridge to get a water sample from the river below. I was working as a water quality technician at the time. It was raining heavily, but I took note when a van approached from the opposite direction and parked across the street about fifty feet away. A logo on the side panel indicated that it belonged to the water district where we worked. Casually I mentioned to Tracy that it must be so-and-so, a fellow employee.

She looked at me quizzically. "That's our company logo on the side of that white van isn't it? I questioned. Her response: "What logo? I don't see any logo."

I squinted my eyes and peered through the downpour. Yes, the van definitely had a blue and white logo, about the size and shape of our water district's. Tracy had youthful eyes. I wondered why she couldn't see such an obvious sign.

We finished our sampling, ran our water quality tests, and quickly loaded our drenched equipment. Driving past the van, I glanced over. I was about to direct Tracy's attention to the logo, and perhaps gloat a little, when I received a shock. The van had no markings at all! Rather than begin a discussion about alternate realities, I simply conceded, "You were right, Tracy. My eyes must have been playing tricks on me."

I'm grateful that the universe began my education of the hologram with small incidents like that one. Who knows how unsettling a spectacular demonstration would have been. But I've read about cases that would likely have unhinged me. For instance, the story of a woman named Tia's miraculous manipulation of reality, as told by Lyall Watson in *Gifts of Unknown Things: A True Story of Nature, Healing, and Initiation from Indonesia's Dancing Island*.[1] This South African scientist, despite numerous academic degrees, found traditional science inadequate in explaining the mysteries of nature. His search for answers led him to remote corners of the globe where he was introduced to the paranormal.[2]

The Disappearing Grove

In *The Holographic Universe* Michael Talbot interprets Watson's experience with respect to holography. He describes Tia's power: "it was consciously controlled and stemmed from Tia's natural connection to forces that lie dormant in most of us." Although Watson had seen Tia use her powers in many ways, Talbot says, the most impressive was not in the presence of an audience.

> Watson witnessed one of Tia's most awesome displays when he accidentally stumbled upon her talking with a little girl in a shady grove of *kenari* trees. Even at a distance, Watson could tell from Tia's gestures that she was trying to communicate something important to the child. Although he could not hear their conversation, he could tell from her air of frustration that she was not succeeding. Finally, she stopped talking, paused, and then started an eerie dance.
>
> Entranced, Watson continued to watch as she gestured toward the trees, and although she scarcely seemed to move, there was something

hypnotic about her subtle gesticulations. Then she did something that both shocked and dismayed Watson. She caused the entire grove of trees suddenly to blink out of existence. As Watson states, "One moment Tia danced in a grove of shady *kenari;* the next she was standing alone in the hard, bright light of the sun."

A few seconds later she caused the grove to reappear, and from the way the little girl leapt to her feet and rushed around touching the trees, Watson was certain that she had shared the experience also. But Tia was not finished. She caused the grove to blink on and off several times as both she and the little girl linked hands, dancing and giggling at the wonder of it all. Watson simply walked away, his head reeling.[3]

Watson's interactions with Tia played a prominent role in *Gifts of Unknown Things*. In the book he reveals how Tia had accomplished her feat. While yet a child, she had learned that our outer reality is constructed by the mind. Watson explains: "She blotted out the image in her mind, and the other trees [in the physical world] vanished with it."[4]

Upon hearing Tia's story I was struck by the fact that those close to the spiritual worlds can manipulate reality so easily. When the Chief first told me the following tale, which can be found in *Autobiography of a Yogi* by Paramahansa Yogananda, it reinforced this point.[5]

A Palace in the Himalayas

Lahiri Mahasaya was an adept in Yogananda's line of teachers. The account details his initial meeting (in this lifetime) with his guru, Babaji, the Ageless Saint, in the autumn of 1861. Lahiri worked as a government accountant. When transferred to the Himalayan post of Ranikhet, his duties allowed him ample time to roam the hills where a number of spiritual masters were said to reside.

On one such outing, Lahiri ascended Drongiri Mountain and found himself at the edge of a small clearing. A number of caves dotted the granite walls flanking the meadow. Lahiri heard someone calling his name. Standing on a rocky ledge near the opening of a cave, his hand extended in welcome, was Babaji!

The adept asked Lahiri if he recognized his surroundings. He did not. Then Babaji struck Lahiri lightly on the forehead. A wondrous current surged through his brain and released the memories of his previous life. During that incarnation he'd spent many years as Babaji's close disciple. This cave had belonged to Lahiri. His bowl, brass cup, and blanket were waiting for him here. Babaji had looked after them. Lahiri then stayed overnight with his teacher and other disciples, sleeping around a campfire outside.

Around midnight Lahiri was roused from sleep by another disciple, who led him on a trek through the forest. In the distance was a luminous glow. His guide explained that the light was the glow from a golden palace. He reminded Lahiri that in the dim past Lahiri had set in motion a desire that had gone unfulfilled—he had dreamed of enjoying the beauties of just such a palace. Tonight, his guide explained, Babaji was fulfilling that wish, thus freeing him from future karma.

Lahiri's description of the palace has become a legend, often recited by his disciples:

A vast palace of dazzling gold stood before us. Studded with countless jewels, and set amidst landscaped gardens, it presented a spectacle of unparalleled grandeur. Saints of angelic countenance were stationed by resplendent gates, half-reddened by the glitter of rubies. Diamonds, pearls, sapphires, and emeralds of great size and luster were imbedded in the decorative arches.

Lahiri's guide explained, ". . . the entire cosmos is a materialized thought of the creator. . . . All its molecules are held together by the will of God. When He withdraws His will, the Earth again will disintegrate into energy. . . ."

He continues:

The substance of a dream is held in materialization by the subconscious thought of the dreamer. When that cohesive thought is withdrawn, the dream and its elements dissolve. A man closes his eyes and erects a dream-creation, which, on awakening, he effortlessly dematerializes. He follows the divine archetypal pattern. Similarly, when he awakens in cosmic consciousness, he will instantly dematerialize the illusions of the cosmic dream.

Being one with the infinite all-accomplishing Will, Babaji can summon the elemental atoms to combine and manifest themselves in any form. . . . Babaji created this palatial mansion out of his mind and is holding its atoms together by the power of his will. . . . When this structure has served its purpose, Babaji will dematerialize it.

As morning approached, Babaji asked Lahiri to close his eyes. When he opened them again, the enchanting palace had vanished. He was now seated on the bare ground with his master and a few disciples, in the exact location where the palace had been.

"'Few mortals know that the kingdom of God includes the kingdom of mundane fulfillments,' Babaji observed. 'The divine realm extends to the earthly, but the latter, being illusory, cannot include the essence of reality.'"

Listening to the Chief tell this story while sitting on the back porch of his cabin one August afternoon, had nurtured my budding interest in exploring the holographic nature of reality. Shortly thereafter I purchased Yogananda's book. Earlier that day I had dropped by the cabin with some huckleberries that I'd picked the day before near Swiftwater Park. Mr. Redstone stirred up some buttermilk pancake batter and I contributed the huckleberries. Some pure maple syrup topped it off nicely. Now, years later, I still associate huckleberry pancakes with our discussion of the hologram.

Consciousness, Energy, and the Cosmic Movie

The Chief often repeated key ideas. For example, he told me time and again how it isn't possible to divide reality into pieces. That took the cooperation of illusion. He said, "True form can only be experienced on the fifth dimension and beyond. In manifesting reality in the dual worlds, it is necessary to take a picture of an idea, then split that picture into opposites on the polarity shaft of a light wave. (But each of the 'copies' contains within it the whole.) This is the function of mind. Light waves are cube shaped vacuum chambers bounded by inert gasses. The idea for television came from the light wave of creation."

From previous discussions, I knew that mind was not the same as consciousness. I asked the Chief how consciousness related to energy.

JR: "Consciousness consists of the energy of love. It is whole; it cannot be divided. It is also still. It contains only the potential of energy. Once an idea is copied and then split into opposites, a polarity is formed. Dynamic energy is created when ideas are split. A rhythmic balanced interchange between the poles keeps the energy in motion.

"By creating the illusion of dividing the One into parts, it is possible to have a wide variety of experiences that would be unavailable to a single being. So, this wonderful game of duality was invented for that purpose. Ideas are set in motion by creator-beings like ourselves. They are then returned to stillness once their purpose has been fulfilled. We could say that energy is consciousness in motion; consciousness is energy that has been returned to stillness."

M: Rather than resembling a solid, inflexible reality, the Chief made it sound more like a 3D movie that we were participating in. He had spoken about two opposing lights that, when projected through one another, create an interference pattern that gives the illusion of reality. Our senses interpret the point where the intersecting waves meet as particles. The brain is the master decoder. It determines that one frequency of waves is a picnic table, another a red and white checkered tablecloth, and yet another, blue sky.

"Then where is the projector and movie screen?" I questioned. [Looking back, this was akin to a character in a 3D movie turning to another character and asking rather indignantly, "If this is a movie we're in, then where is the projector?"]

JR: "Using the example of a movie theater," the Chief answered patiently, "our consciousness would be the light. Sitting facing the front of the theater, we don't see the projector in the back. Similarly, the projector in our own movie lies behind our conscious mind, in the subconscious. Images are projected from the center of our being in the form of waves onto a spherical screen surrounding us. Our brain picks up these waves and assembles them into solid objects."

[The Chief always simplified complicated topics. In this case, however, he would later elaborate that we have *two* projectors, one puts out white light and the other, black light. There are seven colors in black light, just as there are seven colors in white light. By reviewing the Chief's description of the light wave of creation, I was able to form a better picture of the mechanics of holographic projection.

To think out loud for a moment, ideas are expressed, then voided back to stillness. The expression phase would be the white light. The voidance phase would be its opposite, black light. According to Walter Russell, author of *The Secret of Light,* opposites are in actuality different conditions of the very same thing. The cube and the sphere are one and the same. The cube of space is the sphere extended to black coldness; the sphere is the cube compressed to white-hot incandescence. Through rhythmic balanced interchange they become each other. This is the principle of duality at a glance—the cosmic motion picture mechanism.[6]

Time flows in two directions. Our senses pick up the forward movement only. We can't detect the backward flow, which cancels out its forward counterpart. Time is as unreal as the illusory wave universe we occupy.[7] But, like the character in the 3D movie, we can't readily understand this since our senses are part of the illusion.]

JR: "Remember when we talked about the 'Law of Proximity?' Whenever someone comes within our 'sphere of influence,' they must reflect back to us the contents of our Belief System. Our field once radiated out a good 100 feet. But now it's roughly 50 feet." Mr. Redstone smiled mischievously. "It may be that we have to scrunch together these days with the Earth so overcrowded!" [I took this as a joke at the time, but now I'm not so sure.]

The Chief continued. "This could also be the approximate distance our holographic movie screen extends from us. Our universe appears solid, but in reality it is a projected image that blinks on and off billions of times per second. It appears infinite, but as you can see, it is exceedingly finite."

M: "When I got the idea to pick huckleberries yesterday, was that part of a script that somebody wrote? Am I simply acting out a part in a movie? It seemed like the idea came from my own mind at the time."

JR: "Our ideas, intentions, and desires all originate in a deeper part of ourselves, a part that is below the surface of everyday, waking consciousness. Studies have shown that a surge of brain activity takes place about a third of a second before we have a conscious intention to do something."[8]

M: "So, where did I get the idea to pick huckleberries?"

JR: "Our motivations are either fear-based, or they are inspired by love. Those inspired by love come from Wholeness, via our Higher Self. Fear-based responses originate in the Seedbed. Both sources reside beyond our conscious awareness.

"I'd say your desire to pick huckleberries came from Wholeness, but it's difficult to say for sure. Surprisingly, situations that make us uncomfortable often come from Wholeness, too. Take the case of denial. When we deny that we are selfish, for instance, we will see that quality in others, but not in ourselves. Our Higher Self seeks to regain Wholeness. It might arrange situations where we meet that shadow part of ourselves again and again. Until we learn about the Mirror of Life, we will view these experiences as negative.

"When we complain, blame, judge, and deny we resist our return to Wholeness. Our awakening from the movie, as you like to say, gets delayed. But eventually we will come to learn the mechanics of reflection, take responsibility for the unsavory aspects of ourselves we see in others, and welcome those qualities back to love.

"The repository of negativity we call the Seedbed lies below our conscious awareness. Its physical focal point is the third ventricle of the brain. When we began creating more negativity than we could balance in a single lifetime, the hierarchy split off a portion of the mind to act as a repository for this negativity. The ego was appointed to oversee it. Unless we couch our desires in picture form, our thoughts are processed through the belief system to insure that they conform to its contents. This is the outdated survival mechanism that we need to transcend.

"We may hold judgments such as unworthiness in our Seedbed. These judgments become the 'rules we have agreed to live by' until higher understandings take their place. A higher understanding—one put into picture form using the imagination—will transmute all related judgments of lower frequency in the Seedbed. As we have already learned, where there are judgments, we will always find trapped emotions.

"We react unconsciously when an engram is triggered. It may be a sound, smell, taste, memory, or an event that triggers a reaction. Our fight or flight mode kicks in. We hunker down into survival mode. We get a tight, uncomfortable feeling in the pit of our stomach. When we find ourselves in unknown territory, the fear of being hurt or killed is commonly triggered.

"Soul survives, but the body does not. Our cellular memory carries numerous instances where this has been confirmed. These primitive survival fears constitute the Belief System's innermost core. The ego believes that it will cease to exist when the Seedbed is cleared. It will not. It will be reabsorbed into the higher mind where it originated." The Chief drew in a deep breath of crisp river air. He then continued in a lighthearted tone.

"Have a talk with your ego," he advised. "Thank it for supervising the Seedbed with such diligence. Explain to it why you're transmuting the judgments and fears that it looks after so carefully. The ego has done its job of protecting us well. We have survived! But tell it that a transformation is under way; struggling to survive will no longer be necessary.

"Both the ego and the transmuted contents of the Belief System will be taken to a much better place. All of its life it's been surrounded by judgments of unworthiness. Tell the ego that it's worthy of love. Shower it with love. Enlist the ego's help." Mr. Redstone grinned. [I knew he was serious. He advocated talking to your body when it was ill, too.]

"But," the Chief quickly interjected, "the ego is no fool. If we don't do what we've promised—begin loving that which we've denied—the ego will continue to fight us.

"When energy gets 'stuck' it cannot return to Wholeness, or stillness. Therefore, a part of our consciousness remains trapped, as well as our personal power. This is why I keep reiterating the importance of understanding the Belief System." [Two chapters in *Dragon's Breath* are dedicated to the Seedbed and Mirror of Life. A complementary chapter details the Chief's Golden Formula, his approach to clearing out the Seedbed. An additional method has been included in Chapter 9 of this book.]

M: "If this is a cosmic movie, where did the script originate?"

JR: "Yes, it can appear like a movie, can't it? It can also resemble a dream, from which we will eventually awaken. Look at it this way. In the Unchanging Ocean of Ecstasy there is no negativity, absolutely none. Souls dwelling in this abode are part of the Whole, the Realm of All That Is. But, like clouds floating in the sky, there are large gestalts of consciousness in the Ocean of Love. Unlike existence here, however, there are no rain clouds; life is harmonious and perfect.

"Now, imagine a small cube floating in an endless sea of perfect bliss. Only within that tiny cube is it possible to experience anything *other* than ecstasy, joy, and total consciousness. The cube was dreamed into being for the purpose of exploring practically unimaginable ideas, those associated with separation, pain, and hardship. Initially, its creation was likely regarded as a strange, yet revolutionary 'project.' Its value in educating younger Souls in the continuum was no doubt promoted; it would also further God's quest for self-awareness and self-discovery.

"Where did the 'Dreamland script' originate, you asked? I honestly don't know. But I imagine God has the movie rights." The Chief laughed at his quip. "We do believe that it originated in the Realm of All That Is. We also know that ours is one of several 'artificial, multi-dimensional reality matrices.' These 'cubes' may have been created by God, Itself, or by powerful spiritual beings within the highest realms." [I've since learned to view these cubes more like cells within a larger body. Hints of a "cosmic man" have drifted out, but such a notion raises more questions than it answers. It's too big a stretch of the imagination for our current way of thinking.]

M: I excused myself for a necessary break, while the Chief brewed a fresh pot of licorice-root tea. We continued our conversation in the comfort of the living room.

The Dreamland Matrix

JR: "In my mind I sometimes compare the artificial reality of Dreamland to an elaborate computer game. Imagine, if you will, three very bright, but somewhat awkward, heavenly computer programmers. Each evening they meet in a spotless room in a well-kept house in an upscale neighborhood. But, of course, all of the neighborhoods in the Realm of All That Is are upscale!" By the lilt in his voice, I could tell the Chief was enjoying his story.

"During the day these programmers all wear immaculate white uniforms to work. They eat their dinners, prepared perfectly in replicators, at precisely six o'clock each evening. Life is grand; but boredom has driven them to contemplate an outrageous enterprise.

"One night these three brilliant minds come up with a novel idea. They create an interactive game, one in which the players have the freedom to choose between a wide variety of experiences, and not all pleasant. Some of these experiences will be frightening; others will be adventuresome; other choices could lead players into intricate mazes where illusion is intensified. There will be many levels of this game to enjoy and negotiate. Some lower, darker levels will make them wonder if they'll ever find their way out of the illusionary game, back to the reality of their perfect world, the Ocean of Love.

"Beliefs of each player will also shift the reality of the game. [The elite have manipulated the game through religion, politics, and social engineering, to name a few programs.] Choices will determine which roads open up before them. Oh, and there are consequences associated with their choices, too. It's a creative game, you see. By creating without love the game can turn into a living nightmare. One can become completely lost in the game, even forgetting that it's just an illusion.

"Okay, continuing with our analogy, the programmers succeed in creating this challenging holographic game. They call it 'The Dreamland Matrix,' or simply, 'Dreamland.' Others will later refer to it as 'The Matrix.'[9] The Great Councils of Heaven give their approval, and the experiment with polarity begins. The designers of the game bravely send parts of themselves into the game, fragments of their own consciousness." [I remember feeling more comfortable inserting the word "God" in place of "designers." It was easier for me to grasp.]

The Chief paused and stroked his chin. "Each of the three programmers multiply themselves into the multitude of different players in Dreamland, dividing

95

and limiting their consciousness at each of the many levels. A variety of different attributes and abilities are necessary to make the game believable. In the end, if all goes well, the players will awaken from the game. The lessons they learn will go far in furthering God's knowledge of Itself.

M: "I like your analogy. So, are we, as Soul, the programmers, the creators of Dreamland?"

JR: "Perhaps," he said. "But in my contemplations I've seen another possibility. We, meaning our lifewave, entered Dreamland nearly a trillion years ago. When this analogy first came to me, in my inner vision I saw a prior group of Souls exiting this Matrix before we arrived on the scene.

"After experiencing the many wonders of this illusionary game, they found their way out into Reality as planned. Free will was honored by these players. In our case, however, freewill has been subverted by players wanting to highjack the game for their own selfish motives. We're not unique in this. Violation of free will has happened in other 'floating cubes,' as well. It makes the game much more difficult to play."

M: "How do we win the game?"

JR: The Chief was silent for a moment. "The Matrix is balanced so that neither side can win; not the Light; not the Dark. It was designed for experiencing both polarities, and for learning lessons derived from those experiences. Balance swings from one polarity to the other, then back again through unending cycles. But the game itself is designed to always end up a draw.

"A better question might be: How do we get out of the hologram? Or, how do we wake up from this waking dream? Philosophies have been built around these very questions. Most people sleepwalk through life in a hypnotic trance without getting near the truth. They see themselves as nothing more than a physical body. They don't realize they're divine beings playing an illusory game. They're temporarily lost in Dreamland. Knowing that we're living in an artificial-reality matrix certainly gives us an advantage.

"It could be that we play the game until the alarm goes off and it's time to wake up!" The Chief chuckled. "It could be as simple as that. There could be a predetermined time in which this happens. I can't say otherwise.

"But awakening from this illusion appears to take place in many stages. We have to start where we are, not where we'd like to be. Our goal is to remember who we are—Divine Dreamers. We can begin by 'unlearning' who we are not. We strip away the judgments and assumptions that no longer serve us. Self-responsibility, self-acceptance, and self-awareness—mastering (or partially mastering) these steps will take us far toward our monumental moment of awakening.

"Mystics talk about the Music of the Spheres, the current of energy leading back to the Source. By singing HU, or other sacred words, we can tune in to this stream of Light and Sound. Its celestial melodies serve as a cosmic wake-up call, gently nudging us to turn away from the game and return to Wholeness.

JR: "Whatever the method, we must break free of the chains that bind us to the illusion. By cleaning out the Seedbed, or polishing the Mirror of God, the path to the heart begins to open up. Soul begins to catch glimpses of Itself in the world of dreams. We begin to remember once again that 'I AM,' and that 'I always will be.'" The Chief looked out across the twilight meadow at Goldie, his Golden Retriever, who was sniffing her way through the rushes near Little River. She had likely caught wind of the covey of quail we'd seen earlier.

M: "What happens if we get lost in Dreamland and never find our way out?" I squirmed in my chair.

JR: The Chief shook his head. "This can never happen. God has built into the game a failsafe mechanism. At some predetermined point, should the game ever become too far out of balance—too dark and chaotic, God will awaken the players. Dreamland will immediately evaporate into the nothingness that it is. [The Chief often used the pronoun, "He," rather than "Its" when describing God's love.] God loves all players beyond measure, those taking on dark roles, as well. He would never allow His children to endure permanent separation from His endless love."

*   *   *

"The world is nothing more
than an externalized dream.
Whatever the mind believes intensely
immediately comes to pass."

—Paramahansa Yogananda
Autobiography of a Yogi
(1946)[10]

–7–

Birth of the Sat Shatoiya

Seeing the site of the old cabin had brought a rush of memories—times spent talking with the Chief, picking vegetables in his garden, and venturing off on an occasional sightseeing trip. Generally the Chief picked the destination, but one autumn day I suggested an excursion to the Bohemia Basin where an abandoned mining town stood testament to a bygone era. It turned out to be a picture postcard day.

That overcast, late October morning we drove into the mountainous region where a hundred years earlier vast armies of gold seekers had descended (or ascended) to stake their claims. Ruts wider than the tires of our Jeep made the going tough. I'd explored the area several years earlier with an acquaintance from the mill who had introduced me to gold panning. Since then, the road had taken a turn for the worse. With almost a mile to go before reaching our destination, the road became impassable. Wrapping scarves tightly around the neckline of our winter jackets, we parked at a wide area and continued on foot.

Colorful maples, alders, and birches splashed the hillsides with reds, golds, yellows, and oranges. Pine, spruce, and Douglas fir lent the palate their green and blue-green hues. A covey of quail darted across the brushy roadway ahead of us in their comical, zigzag pattern. It was as if the lead quail had been plagued with indecision. His followers raced after him frantically, anxiously clucking their mounting concerns. "For heaven's sake," they admonished, "please make up your mind!"

Breathing in the fresh mountain air gave my body a burst of vigor. I remember feeling so alive and exhilarated when we crested the top of a ridge and came face to face with the old mining town. Not often was the Chief surprised, but on this particular day his voice trailed off in amazement. "Would you look at that!"

Dilapidated old buildings lined a broad dirt strip that had once served as Main Street. The post office sign still beckoned from its position above the entry, although a hundred years had passed since a customer had ventured in. A stagecoach building peeked out from beneath giant willow bows. It had been abandoned by man; only sparrows and wrens now called it home. Noisy Blue Jays were unwelcome. They watched over the bank, just a few doors down.

A collapsed building, now only a pile of rotting lumber, sprawled out in the center of town—a hotel perhaps. For almost an hour the Chief and I went our separate ways, taking in the unusual spectacle. I finally ran into the Chief again in the tiny sheriff's office. He was enjoying the view through a hole in the wall where a window had been. The ancient police station sat perched on a ridge—the highest point in town—overlooking the hillside beyond the ravine. The vantage point provided a clear view of the road below, the only accessible way in or out of town.

Something happened next that made the surreal sensation of stepping outside of time that day even more memorable. It began to snow. Thanksgiving generally ushered in the first snowfall in the mountains of Oregon, so this early gift was a rare treat. The Chief and I glanced at each other approvingly. Nothing was said. We just drank in the moment: the falling flakes of snow, the colorful trees decorating the hillside, the forgotten mining town—a remnant from the past—and the company of friends. My everyday life simply vanished, much like the prospectors who had abandoned these buildings when the gold had run out.

As a middle-aged man, Mr. Redstone had owned and operated several mining claims, mostly in the Steamboat area, a few miles northwest as the crow flies. I'm sure my friend and mentor's mind was churning with memories from that time in his life. The word "Steamboat" can be traced to the early gold miners. "In the miners' parlance of the day, if an area did not come up to expectations, or claims had been fraudulently sold to unsuspecting newcomers, the miners leaving the scene were said to have 'steamboats' out of the area."[1] The Chief rarely talked about his accomplishments, or lack thereof, in the gold mining field; but considering his track record in other endeavors, it was likely a big success.

Steamboat never became an important mining destination, unlike the Bohemia Basin area. This quaint mining town, stranded high in the mountains, was a testament to that. While we gazed out upon the falling snow, the Chief began a discourse on success.

JR: "Some miners struck it rich here, Michael. Most did not, of course. When I think of success, it's not something measured in gold, though." The Chief pointed to

101

the hillside just below us where a buck deer was testing the wind. Steam was rising from his nostrils.

"Did we love? Did we serve? Did we accomplish what we came to Earth to do? I suspect that's what we'll be asked when we cross over to the other side. If we did these three things, then our lives were totally success-ful; if not, then we should have tried a little harder."

M: "How will I know what I've come here to do? There's no book on the subject, is there?" I was being cute. I didn't really expect an answer.

JR: "That would be way too easy, now, wouldn't it?" The Chief grinned. "But yes, actually, there are many good books that give us clues. Since each person's life is different, there are no one-size-fits-all templates available. We have to figure much of it out on our own through self-examination.

The Hero's Journey

JR: "Joseph Campbell wrote a book called *The He-ro's Journey.*[2] Campbell discovered that each individu-al's life contains a personal legend, a story containing within it all the archetypes of the hero's journey."

[As the Chief began explaining the archetypal play-ers that show up in our lives, I immediately thought of a Hollywood movie. Screenwriters know that a script must contain specific elements, ones that have made previous movies successful at the box office.

Later in life I found a copy of Campbell's book mis-filed in the poetry section of a library, and began study-ing the elements of myth in greater detail. Without the Chief's overview that day in the Bohemia Basin, how-ever, I doubt that I would have given the book a second glance.]

JR: "By studying the great myths of the world, and by examining his own life and the lives of others, Campbell discovered that each person has his or her own personal myth. He found that a small group of root symbols, or 'archetypes,' kept showing up across the board, although outward experiences varied from person to person. These symbols originate in the unconscious." As the Chief was talking, I tried to connect the mythical archetypes with events and people in my own life. Of course some of the puzzle pieces were missing; my life was still unfolding at the time.

JR: "For example, Campbell found that every myth begins with a **call to adventure**. Many times it is an unexplainable experience that launches the individual on a search for life's answers. The call always comes at a significant time in a person's life, at a crossroads. In mythical terms, crossroads are known as 'thresholds.'

"When the adventurer/hero gets the call, which could be an invitation to study metaphysics, let's say, he finds himself at the boundary of a new region. Beyond his present comfort zone lies the great unknown. At this point, the ego will step forward and remind the adventurer what could happen if he continues onward. To the ego, the choice comes down to a simple mathematical equation: the unknown = possible death.

"When the adventurer approaches the edge of the great unknown, it triggers a confrontation with the **Guardian of the Threshold**. This individual or social group is the outward manifestation of the ego. It is his (or their) duty to point out that lions and tigers await one so foolish as to stray beyond the safety of the popular religion or 'acceptable social behavior.' The jungle is a dangerous place!

"No good can come from leaving the flock and plunging into the labyrinth of the unknown. You'll recognize threshold guardians by their concerned cry, 'What if?' What if you go out there and can't find your way back? What if people think you've gone mad? What if the preacher finds out?"

[My kind old grandmother, bless her heart, faithfully fulfilled her role as my threshold guardian. She meant well, of course. "What if the Devil is behind all this metaphysics?" she would ask fearfully. All my reassurances didn't help. Her own threshold guardians had been quite successful at keeping her chained to her rigid beliefs.]

JR: "Campbell goes on to say that two things can happen at this point. If the adventurer is frozen in fear, or shows no interest in moving forward, this constitutes a **refusal of the call**. It indicates a reluctance on the part of Soul to forge ahead. But if the desire to awaken is strong enough, there will be an **acceptance of the call**.

"The **passage of the threshold** leading to the **labyrinth** represents a form of self-annihilation. At this point, let's call the adventurer the hero, for he's now in the game. The hero of myth journeys inward and is symbolically 'swallowed up in the belly of the whale.' This begins the **road of trials**, which ultimately leads to the **treasure**."

[The labyrinth of myth is generally depicted as a desert, an uncharted sea, or as a dark forest. The Chief used the example of a jungle. The labyrinth represents our inner universe; specifically, our own Seedbed, or Belief System.]

JR: "Campbell writes about an archetype called the **meeting with the Goddess**. In psychology it's called integrating our anima/animus, our complementary half. The anima is the feminine principle residing in the unconscious of the male; the animus is the male principle within the unconscious of women." [The Chief wasn't able to elaborate much on this archetype, other than the fact that Carl Jung, the psychologist, had coined the term. I gathered, however, that the meeting with the goddess is important in returning to Wholeness.]

"The **Adversary** is an interesting character. On our journey to Wholeness, which is really the same as the hero's journey, we come up against resistance. It's built into the game to test our strength and resolve. Jung also coined another term, the 'shadow.' The shadow represents the negative qualities and fears we have pushed into denial. We don't want anyone to see this side of ourselves, and we certainly don't want to view ourselves in a negative manner. Once again we resist. But the shadow needs healing. We do this with understanding, acceptance, and with love."

M: "Where does the shadow reside?"

JR: "It is hidden in the Seedbed, or Belief System. Oh, we occasionally catch glimpses of it reflected in other people, but its creation and ultimate transformation is totally our responsibility."

[That "R" word seemed to come up a lot. I've been asked, "What is the most important thing you learned from the Chief?" Without a doubt, it's the information about the Belief System and the Mirror of Life. But, equally important, the Chief was a great role model and friend. As he put it, he was simply sharing with others what had helped him. He didn't watch you like a hawk to see how you used his information. That's why, when he mentioned the next archetype, I immediately thought of him.]

JR: "Fortunately we have helpers on our journey through the labyrinth. The hero must walk the path for himself, but a **Supernatural Aide** will appear to offer direction and guidance. The supernatural aide is often portrayed as a wise old man or a fairy godmother. In real life, however, this is generally a spiritual teacher. Over the course of a lifetime we may have a number of teachers who fit this description. All point us in the direction of Wholeness."

[From this I gathered that we would cross many minor thresholds on our journey. These "initiations" would each represent a minor awakening. The **Great Awakening** of myth would likely correspond to the realization that we are part of God.

The Chief passed over an archetype called the **Mystic Marriage**. To be honest, I can only speculate on it. Soul is said to join with Divine Spirit in a mystical sense at some point in the journey back to Wholeness. Perhaps this takes place when Soul first leaves duality on its way to greater heights. By cleaning out the Seedbed and reabsorbing the ego into the higher mind, Soul prepares for this union.]

JR: "Once the hero successfully traverses the road of trials he discovers the **treasure**. This is often portrayed as a chest of gold, a "Golden Fleece," the rainbow's end, caves filled with precious gems, etc."

[I thought of the 1963 movie, "Jason and the Argonauts," and the struggles Jason had to overcome in reaching the Golden Fleece—the menacing Harpies, the Clashing Rocks, and the skeleton warriors born of the Hydra's teeth.]

JR: "I relate the struggles of myth to our facing and transmuting of the Seedbed. Our return to Wholeness, God-Realization, Love, Reality, whatever you want to call it, is the reward for our efforts. The path ultimately ends in the heart. Awakening from the illusion and finding love to be our own true self is the ultimate prize."

After our discussion, the Chief and I left the sheriff's office and began our descent down the snow-covered pathway leading toward civilization. I glanced around for one last look. Perhaps this abandoned town represented a symbol in my quest for the treasure. If so, it wasn't readily apparent. Although we didn't discuss the remaining archetype that day, there was another challenge remaining for the hero to negotiate. It was called **the return**.

Upon claiming the treasure, once again the hero had to take his place in the world of men. Often he was called upon to become a teacher, to share what he had discovered. But in his absence everything had changed. The hero now found that he was the only one who was truly awake; everyone else was fast asleep.

At last we reached the Jeep, now covered in a blanket of snow. During the Chief's discussion a question had arisen. Rather than interrupt his presentation, I had decided to ask it later. As the Jeep was warming up, I happened to remember it.

M: "I thought the Great Awakening would be the end of the journey. How does it differ from the treasure?"

JR: "Going back to the computer game analogy, I would say that finding the treasure represents finishing the game. We exit the tiny cube and once more find our true identity—a drop of love in the Unchanging Ocean of Ecstasy. We are free of the illusion forever.

"The Great Awakening takes place in the higher levels of the game, but nonetheless, still within the game. As we clean out the Belief System more and more, we begin to catch glimpses of something beyond our ordinary dream reality. By polishing the Mirror of God, a glimmer of light begins to shine through. That light is our true self, Soul.

[The Chief called this "shining through" the birth of the *Sat Shatoiya*. It is the moment when the Divine first recognizes Itself in the world of dreams, the hologram. *Sat* means 'true' in Sanskrit. *Shatoiya* can be traced to "Chatoyancy," a gemstone term.[3] It relates to light—the way it shimmers, dances, and reflects. The Great Awakening is the point at which the true reflection of the Divine begins to light up our consciousness.]

Trials of the Labyrinth

I've never forgotten that snowy October day in the Bohemia Basin. The white flakes of snow superimposed against the colorful hillside were candy to my eyes. The tranquil scene was a snapshot of beauty and joy. Even today, I go back to it in my mind from time to time when life gets overwhelming.

Besides Campbell's work, I found other clues conveniently positioned in my path, ones that pointed to my purpose here on Earth. I can't recall what possessed me to do it, but one day I set aside an hour to evaluate my life thus far, what I'd accomplished, what I still needed to work on. An hour was actually more than enough time; my list of successes was short. I'd start with that.

I scribbled down two things immediately, tests that I'd passed, barriers that I've overcome. The biggest challenge had been my fear of public speaking. Although I hadn't become a Dale Carnegie or Tony Robbins, my modest list of speaking engagements entitled me to be called a speaker. One evening in Chicago, however, my self-confidence was nearly destroyed. The crisis threatened to bring the momentum I had accrued to a screeching halt.

My talk at the large spiritual seminar was scheduled for 7:00 p.m. I was first on the program. A relaxed, somewhat humorous presentation was needed to set the tone for the evening. At 6:15 p.m., minutes before I was to check in at the backstage corral, I huddled in my room in total panic. My mind was racing; my palms were sweating; I couldn't remember a single word of my 15-minute presentation. My usual pre-talk routine had not worked.

I threw myself on the hotel room bed and poignantly asked for help. It came within seconds. A most calming, joyous, golden energy enveloped me. The current of love immediately swept away every bit of anxiousness, doubt, and fear. My mind cleared. It was my first real taste of Divine Love. I wanted to feel that way forever. That entire evening I basked in the afterglow of that joy. It turned out to be the best presentation I had made to date.

The second challenge I'd overcome had been alcohol addiction. It wasn't accomplished overnight, but it was an "overnight success." One day I simply woke up and didn't want any part of it anymore. Most of the credit goes to the Chief for teaching me about the Seedbed and the Golden Formula.

A third great challenge came to mind, but I'd pushed that one far down on my list. Ironically, it was the most important of all. But until I'd built a foundation for tackling it, a staging area on higher ground so to speak, there was little use in setting my sights on that distant star. That was opening the heart and loving myself; specifically, loving myself the way God loved me. But, as Meatloaf so wisely said, "two out of three ain't bad." I was satisfied with that for now. After all, I had a few more good years left to devote to the third challenge, as well as a host of minor ones.

It wasn't but a week after I'd made my list that the universe dropped a book in my lap, a book the Chief had mentioned in passing—Alice Bailey's, *A Treatise on the Seven Rays, Vol. II.*[4] She writes that white light is divided into the seven colors of the spectrum. Qualities and characteristics are inherent to each of the seven rays. [A brief description of the rays was given in *Porcupines at the Dance.*] Each of the various bodies of man comes into being on one of the rays.

It was fairly easy to figure out that my Soul Ray was blue because I enjoy teaching, one of the attributes of the second ray, the Ray of Love/Wisdom. Soul can only come into existence on one of the three primary rays: red, blue, or yellow. But other bodies run the gamut of all seven. There are both strengths and weaknesses associated with each ray. Each person will possess valuable skills, but will encounter various obstacles to be overcome.

When I read about the Fourth Ray, the Ray of Art (my personality ray), I was stunned.[5] Listed as qualities to be gained were the exact three things I had scribbled down on paper not long before. These were self-confidence (public speaking), self-control (alcohol addiction), and an attitude of giving, which I interpreted to mean opening the heart. This was verification that I was on the right track, not lost in the labyrinth of illusion, but moving forward in the direction of the treasure.

No doubt other artists and writers were experiencing similar trials. I wondered how many different legends were possible. Fifth-Ray builders likely had their own personal myths that were similar in nature. The same would be true of Third-Ray businessmen, First-Ray policemen, and so forth. Since there were seven rays, I assumed there would be seven legends of Soul. But another possibility sprang to mind.

Paul Twitchell writes about twelve major life experiences in *The ECK Vidya*.[6] These twelve *nidana*s of the "Wheel of Life" provide Soul with a variety of different opportunities. If the seven rays tell us "why we're like what we are like," the twelve *nidana*s tell us "why we're going through what we are going through." All in all, eighty-four myths could be possible (7 Rays x 12 *nidana*s).

For example, in a *nidana* of conflict such as a war experience, a Third-Ray engineer might be called upon to design a bridge. Should a Fourth-Ray artist find himself in that setting, he might become a war correspondent. A First-Ray general would send men into battle. In the same *nidana*, these three individuals would have very different experiences.

The Missing Archetype

Before leaving the subject of myth, one last point warrants examination. Unless I'm mistaken, Joseph Campbell left out an important archetype. When the adventurer closes in on his prize, the universe tests him to determine his courage and worthiness. This honor falls to the **Guardian of the Treasure**.

111

At the core of the Belief System lie two powerful fears: the fear that we won't survive, and the fear that we will never be worthy of God's love. The tests designed specifically for us by the Guardian of the Treasure will reflect these fears. But by the time we have reached this stage of our journey through the labyrinth, we will have built up the stamina and self-knowledge to accept these challenges in stride. Our meeting with the Guardian may come even before the treasure is in sight.

The **test of courage** could involve risk. Are we willing to place ourselves in harms way to help another? We could be placed in a dangerous situation to see if we are willing to take the next step spiritually. The test may take the form of a life or death drama, or it could simply be a question of inner strength and integrity: are we strong enough to be totally honest in the face of ridicule, alienation, or shame? Will we stand up for what's honorable and right when the masses have chosen the easy way out? The bottom line is this: have we conquered fear?

The **test of worthiness** is perhaps the final barrier between the hero and the treasure. If it feels right, give yourself this practice test. Imagine yourself in a darkened room. Oil-burning lamps, positioned high on each wall, cast eerie shadows. The stone floor and dark, boarded walls give the room a medieval feel. A large block of granite rests near the center of the room.

As you approach the stone, a glimmer of light catches your attention. It is coming from a metal object protruding from the surface of the stone. It looks like the top half of a silver cross. Closer examination reveals it to be the handle of a sword. But this is no ordinary sword. Its blade is imbedded in the block of granite.

112

From out of the ethers comes a voice. It is more like an impression: "Love is the greatest power in the universe. It has no equal. Step forward and see if thou art worthy of the power of love. Step forward and pull the sword from the block of stone."

*   *   *

"Where your heart is,
there you will find your treasure."

—Paulo Coelho
The Alchemist (1988)[7]

–8–

Farewell

From my position on the rough-hewn bench overlooking Colliding Rivers, I could see a thin stream of cars and trucks passing by on Highway 138. On my way through, I'd noticed a new coffee shop beside the gas station just up the road. It was called the "Coffee Hut," or something like that. So many coffee stands had sprung up lately that picking a name was becoming a problem. Soon there'd be nothing left but "Grounds for Divorce," and "See You Latte."

Occasionally a car would pull into the viewpoint, but none fit the description of Marilyn Waters' silver sedan. She had indicated in her note that she'd be driving an older model Mercedes. It was nice of her to chauffer the Chief. I took out the note and reread the neatly printed words again. The Chief had requested my presence at 2:30 p.m. on Saturday, March 24th—today. That was just fifteen minutes away!

With April just around the corner, the Pacific Salmon would be passing through Colliding Rivers on their way upriver. Their destination? The many tributaries of the Umpqua, the place of their birth years before. Steamboat Creek was the largest tributary. On that waterway alone I counted twelve smaller ones.

For many years the Chief had been making an annual pilgrimage to a special place along Steamboat Creek. It was a deep pool located about seven miles northwest of the confluence to the Umpqua. In September of 1989 he invited me to accompany him.

By this time of year, mornings had donned their silver-frost wardrobe. Leaves were changing to their autumn colors. Three hundred-fifty to four hundred salmon sought out this pool in Steamboat Creek during the hot summer months. Because of its depth, it stayed a degree or two cooler than other parts of the river. Soon, with September's recent arrival, the salmon would be leaving. They would strike out on the final leg of their journey to fulfill their destiny. Arriving in the shallow gravel beds of Steamboat's tributaries, their mission would end. They would die after spawning.

To protect the salmon from intruders, a Forest Service Ranger was dispatched to watch over the deep pool each year from April until the salmon left in late September. This put a stop to illegal poaching. Before this, thoughtless intruders using dynamite had decimated the pool; hence the name, "Dynamite Hole."

The Chief's compassionate nature was a stark contrast to the insensitivity, even cruelty, of some of the county's residents. Because of his belief in noninterference, I initially thought the Chief was a bit too detached. He preferred to "allow life to happen" without undue interference. For example, he often remarked: "I wouldn't walk across the street to help anyone." He would pause for effect, and then add with a gleam in his eye, "But I would go to the other side of the world to help someone who asked for my help."

116

Mr. Redstone had a keen mind and a good imagination. Not that he was unloving in any way, but his approach to life leaned more toward wisdom. He was quick to point out, however, that wisdom and love are intimately connected. More than once the Chief had quoted Hazrat Inayat Khan: "In reality wisdom is love and love is wisdom, although in one person wisdom may be predominant and in another love."[1] Both of these paths begin and end in the heart. In case there's any doubt, this is where the treasure lies.

The Heart of the River

The scene was surreal. Just off the Steamboat Creek Road we came upon a tiny trailer perched on the brink of a cliff overlooking the river. A Ranger and his Black Lab greeted us at the edge of his campsite. Even early in the afternoon, the pool was partially shaded by the hillside behind it. My eyes lit up in amazement and disbelief. Hundreds of salmon rolled and churned in the deep pool below us, apparently oblivious to their most recent admirers. The Chief greeted the Ranger as an old friend. I was always impressed at how easily the Chief interacted with others.

Although the Chief never talked about it in these terms, "living from the heart," it embodied how he lived. Some call it "living with grace." After we had climbed down to the lower observation ledge, I asked the Chief how he had arrived at the place where life had become so effortless. Speaking in a quiet tone, he shared some insights he'd learned on his journey from the head to the heart, the shortest, but most difficult journey a person can make.

JR: "I marvel at the cycles of life. These salmon were once tiny fry. In time they made their way to the ocean, where, in a few short years, they experienced untold adventures. One day, however, they began to feel a divine discontent. A memory began to surface, and with it, an urge to set forth from the boundless sea. It was an urge to go home.

"Everything begins in the heart, just as, in time, everything returns to the heart. This pool is sacred. It is the beacon that guided these salmon home. You see, this deep pool is the heart of the river! Every season I return here to honor the new arrivals and celebrate their great accomplishment, their return to the heart."

> Leaves are falling in the path,
> red and yellow, crisp and brittle.
> The way must be prepared.
> A silver tide sweeps through
>   a shallow stream.
> The salmon have returned. They roll
>   and churn
> awaiting one who comes, to sanctify,
> to bless the ancient rite.
> Through crackling leaves he comes,
> then says the words.
> A weathered face surveys the moonlit pool,
> as if he knows . . .
> A coyote cries. A cold wind blows.
> What only lives, can only die.

JR: "At some point we all hear the call to adventure. It is the call to traverse the road of trials and return to our own heart. It is the gentle shake of the master of the house telling us that it's time to wake up. We've dreamed of traveling exotic lands, of meeting kings, of writing books, composing symphonies. We've battled formidable foes across myriad galaxies. In dreams we've dressed as knights, we've bartered as merchants, drifted as vagabonds. But we are not the knight; we are not the merchant; nor are we the vagabond; we have no castles, no enemies, and no goods to buy or sell. The truth is, we have never left our beds!

"Our desire to awaken sets in motion a sequence of events that takes us through the labyrinth and home to the treasure of myth. It's different for each of us, as our dreams have all been different; yet, it's the same. The layers of dreams begin to dissipate like a morning mist when the sun comes out.

"Our core beliefs and judgments are kin to lamp shades, or layers of an onion. These make up the working level of the Belief System. We've talked about balancing all that we've created outside of love. Some call this 'working off karma.' On numerous occasions we've discussed how to recognize limiting judgments and core fears. But what about our core assumptions about ourselves, the things we attach to 'I AM?'

"We can come to believe any number of things that shape how we see ourselves: 'I AM a happy person,' 'I AM worthwhile,' 'I AM a sinner,' 'I AM an American,' 'I AM a slow learner,' 'I AM going to heaven,' 'I AM a victim.' The list is nearly endless. We may be American in this life, but we may have been Chinese in another. We may be handsome in this life; but we may have been something less before. Change appears to be the only constant here in the hologram. But there is one common denominator that does not change: I AM! Once we understand that I AM is the only true constant, then we can begin to let go of the adornments and trappings that distort our view of reality and block our light. These, for the most part, constitute barriers to love."

[I would later uncover two closely-held core beliefs that originated early in life: "I AM unappreciated," and "I AM unworthy of love." These affected the way I viewed myself, and also the way I treated others. It was painful having to look deeply within myself where these false assumptions had limited my ability to love. If you haven't already done so, get a copy of *You Can Heal Your Life,* by Louise Hay.[2]]

JR: "When we operate from the head, the domain of the Belief System, we mistakenly think that by letting go of our judgments and assumptions there will be nothing left. It's something like watching a boring movie and hoping that it never ends, for if it ends, all of life will be extinguished! This fear keeps us in the theater; similarly, false assumptions about who we are keep us trapped in Dreamland.

"We must surrender our most cherished beliefs, as well as any painful memories and limiting fears. In doing so, the pathway leading to the heart begins to open up as if by magic." The Chief shied away from organized teachings, but admitted that others often benefited from structured settings. He warned that many organizations use fear and control to sustain memberships. I had to agree with him on that point. He advocated using contemplation to get his own answers. He looked upon cleaning out the Seedbed as his top priority.

JR: "At the innermost level of the Seedbed is the core belief that we originally had to adopt in order to foster the illusion of separation from the Divine. Our original core assumption? 'I AM separate from God.'

That was the original barrier. Imagine all the debilitating judgments that have arisen over time from imagining that we're separate from All That Is. When we forgot that it had been our own decision to construct this initial barrier, another judgment arose: 'God has abandoned us.' We began to blame God, or (equally as destructive) began to feel unworthy of God, and unworthy of love. Are you beginning to see what must be surrendered in order to enter the heart and return to Unity Consciousness? These core judgments and false assumptions keep us in the head."

M: "Yes, I'm finally getting the picture. When people talk about living in the head as opposed to the heart, they are really talking about the Seedbed. By cleaning out the Seedbed, by whatever method one adopts, the barriers that keep us away from the heart (and love) will eventually come down."

The Chief had walked the same road that I was now negotiating. It was a godsend to have a friend and mentor who had found his way through the labyrinth. He shared a few keys that could make the journey easier.

Approaching the Heart

JR: "People who live from the heart have acquired two healthy qualities: they are honest with themselves and others, and they take full responsibility for their lives. They live simply, love generously, care deeply, and speak kindly. The manner in which they conduct their lives is a direct result of cleaning out the Belief System, or polishing the Mirror of God.

"At first our Belief System dominates—we react to life. That's why it is sometimes called the 'reactive mind.' But the more we clean and polish, the more love and light begins to shine through from the heart. The more freedom we enjoy.

"The path to Oneness, or Reality, runs through the heart. The outer world of the hologram is but a pale reflection. Since it is shaped by our beliefs, you can see the importance of moving beyond outdated paradigms. Through entertainment, media, education, and religion, we are inundated with programming aimed at keeping us asleep and in bondage. Should we wake up to the truth about our divine creative abilities, the hidden hand of the global elite would instantly be lifted."[3]

M: "Those who seek global domination have done everything in their power to keep us in a continual state of ignorance and fear. Where does forgiveness fit in? At one time you said that masters didn't need to forgive. That sounded a little harsh. But then you went on to explain that masters never see themselves as victims; therefore, they never harbor feelings of anger or resentment. There is nothing for them to forgive. Can you elaborate on this?"

JR: "The man on the street has little or no knowledge of the Seedbed. Many could be called 'walking victims,' holding grudges and resentment when they feel wronged or mistreated. These feelings and judgments bolster the negativity in the Seedbed. Forgiveness can be a powerful tool for balancing the Seedbed when it is imbued with love. Love does the balancing with its powerful vibration.

"Anger and resentment are forms of resistance. When we resist anything we give it power. Finding these two negative emotions within us tells us that we once fell into the trap of blame. We missed the opportunity to gracefully balance something we had created outside of love. Instead of using love and forgiveness to zero out the energies, we kept them bottled up and tightly secured. By doing this, we magnetically attracted similar experiences. An understanding of the Seedbed is the foundation for moving out of the head and into the heart.

"Another key is imagination. When we use mental pictures instead of thought, we bypass the reactive mind, or the Belief System. Our Higher Self examines the object of our attention from its lofty position. Solutions to problems aren't always apparent. Since we've been temporarily disconnected from this higher part of ourselves, we have to trust that the answers will be there when needed." [Waking Dreams are one of the ways in which information from our Higher Self is transferred to our 3D reality; others are dreams, intuition, and knowingness.]

"In addition to forgiveness, imagination, and an understanding of the Seedbed, surrender can be a valuable tool in approaching the heart. At some point we must stop fighting against the current and allow life to carry us forward without complaining. The universe works for our highest good; life happens *for* us, not *to* us.

"Instead of chewing on problems, we can use the imagination to assist in surrendering them. After taking responsibility for their creation and balancing them with love and understanding, we can toss our problems into an imaginary fire. We can also release them into a pair of cloud-like hands and see them dissolve. Cleaning out our garages, homes, and our wardrobes frees up space for new, heart-centered energies. We must also be willing to let go of people, places, and habits from our past. This includes those cherished beliefs that no longer serve us.

"Gratitude is a quality dear to the heart. Being thankful fosters an attitude that not only cushions our journey of trials, it actually delivers us to the door of the heart. Every day I find something to be grateful for."

[Earlier in my life I'd been taught the value of gratitude. When I'd worked briefly in real estate development and sales, my brother and I had leased an office next door to a business that made prosthetics. One day I was leaving our office in a foul mood over a trivial matter involving a potential buyer who had changed his mind. As I approached my shiny red sports car, I noticed a young woman getting out of an old Pinto. She was struggling with a pair of metal crutches. These attached to her forearms, thereby lending support when she walked. As we passed in the parking lot she gazed up at me, her face beaming with joy. "Good morning!" she greeted, in the most delightful, lilting voice.

I was stunned. I had expected to meet a person beaten down by life. Her buoyant attitude lifted my spirits immediately. I was also ashamed. There was so much to be thankful for, yet I was scowling and complaining about insignificant matters. For the longest time I sat silently in my car digesting what had happened. This young woman became my hero, as well as a most important teacher. She taught me the importance of gratitude. Whenever I ran into speed bumps in my life after that, I would always remember this young girl with her million-dollar attitude.]

Sanctuary of the Heart

JR: "Permission must be granted in order to enter the sacred realm of the heart." The Chief glanced down at the river below us as a shadow traced its way across the surface of the pool. An osprey patrolling for an easy meal, perhaps?

"Who do we ask?" the Chief questioned rhetorically. "We ask ourselves! Our I AM Presence dwells in the fifth chamber of the heart, on the supra-physical level. Some call this the 'high heart.' If we could magnify the I AM Presence millions of times, we would find the most beautiful, youthful likeness of ourselves encased in a translucent sphere of light. Three flames imbued with love, wisdom, and power radiate from this divine image of ourselves. Its function is to magnetically record our every thought, feeling, and action.

"The I AM Presence awaits in the sanctuary of the heart. This sacred space molds itself to our thoughts; therefore, our sanctuary may take any shape we imagine. Since our favorite places 'out here in the hologram' are reflections of inner realities, we can choose how the sanctuary of the heart will appear. Think of your favorite places for a moment." My favorite hike led along Fall Creek to a beautiful waterfall. The Chief picked this as an example.

JR: "Say you choose Fall Creek. Picture the scene clearly in your mind—the mist from the falls, sunlight peeking through firs flanking the massive rock walls, birds chirping, etc. Imagine your I AM Presence waiting for you near the base of the falls. Before you start up the pathway, be sure and ask permission to enter the sacred space of the heart.

"The radiant form of your I AM Presence is seated in lotus fashion on a patch of green grass beside the water. As you approach from the trail, you are struck by the beauty and light emanating from this majestic being. You are welcomed with opened arms, with love

125

and acceptance. From this point forward your energies and consciousness will intermingle. You will know that you are worthy of two precious treasures: the treasures of God and the treasures of man."

Meeting Marilyn Waters

My reverie of Fall Creek and my I AM Presence was interrupted when a silver car pulled into the far end of the parking lot. The driver was an older woman, but she was alone. A second car pulled in and parked beside her. A couple of teenagers jumped out and bounded across the street in the direction of the Information Center. I glanced at my watch. It was two-thirty five.

I began flipping through my list of contacts on my phone, and was about to call an old softball friend when I heard someone approaching the bench where I was seated from behind. Startled, I turned to find a slender, grey-haired woman wearing a black sweater and dark grey slacks. "Are you Michael?" she asked.

Rising to my feet, I glanced back across the parking lot. The kids had gone, and I could now see the Mercedes emblem on the remaining car quite clearly. "You must be Marilyn," I answered, extending my hand to greet her. "It's a pleasure to finally meet you in person." She ignored my offering and, instead, leaned in and gave me a warm hug.

"It was nice of you to come," she told me. "John has spoken of you so often that I feel like I know you. Would you walk with me to the car?" I nodded, thinking to myself that I'd probably find the Chief napping in the back seat. He enjoyed his naps. More than once he'd drifted off while I'd driven back from an outing.

126

My first memories of Ms. Waters had come from an old black and white photograph the Chief had displayed at his cabin. The two of them had been standing by a canoe, one the Chief had made. For the Chief, paddling a canoe was an "inherited skill." Although he never came right out and said it, I got the impression that Mr. Redstone had once lived as Captain Clark. Canoes had been a major mode of transportation during the Lewis and Clark Expedition.

The snapshot of Ms. Waters had been taken when she had been quite young, in her late twenties, as I remembered. In the picture she'd appeared delicate, but attractive. The Chief rarely spoke about his past, but from fragments here and there I could tell that he had shared the best part of his life with this frail, elderly woman now walking beside me. I never did know if they'd been married. I'd felt awkward asking. But I knew that he loved her.

When I'd spoken with the Chief about five months earlier, he'd been living in a retirement community in a suburb of Portland. He'd mentioned that Ms. Waters had been helping him with some personal matters. I'd suggested getting together again, maybe even at Colliding Rivers, if he felt up to it. I had offered to buy him lunch at "Munchies." It hadn't occurred to me that Ms. Waters would be joining us; but of course, she was more than welcome.

Now, as we approached the car, I couldn't help but think how surreal this long overdue meeting between the three of us seemed. When Ms. Waters opened the rear driver's side door I could see books and some raingear in the seat, but the Chief apparently hadn't come with her. How curious, I thought. I wondered if he'd decided to take his own car at the last minute. He still had friends in the area. Perhaps he was planning to visit with them afterwards. Ms. Waters removed a cardboard box from the seat and gently handed it to me. There was something metallic inside, a container of some kind.

There are moments in your life that are frozen in time. As I took the box, I remember the churning of the river below us, the crispness of the air, the chattering of a blue jay scolding the intruders below him from the oak tree above us . . . and I vividly remember suppressing an involuntary gasp. Ms. Waters placed a reassuring hand on my shoulder. Somehow I managed to gather myself. I knew now that the Chief would not be coming in his own car. He had already arrived. And this would be his last trip to Colliding Rivers. The brass container was an urn.

Ms. Waters explained that the Chief had contacted her when he'd become ill. She'd helped him wrap up his affairs and had found a home for his old car, a man down on his luck. The Chief had passed on recently due to congestive heart failure. Per his instructions, his body had been cremated. His final wish was to return to Colliding Rivers. Here, his ashes would be scattered by the two people he loved the most. I was honored to have been his friend. It was also an honor to be present now for his farewell ceremony.

I was struck by the lack of fanfare. A great Soul had passed, and the world went on the same as it did every other day. It had stopped only for Ms. Waters and for me. There were no brass bands, no speeches, and no memorials other than the ones the two of us held silently in our minds. She placed her hands affectionately on the urn, while I supported it and removed the lid. A stiff breeze took the grey-white ashes over the embankment toward the river. They trembled briefly on the wind, and then they were gone. They vanished into the mist above Colliding Rivers.

Ms. Waters left shortly thereafter. I respected her need to be alone. I felt the same way. For a good half hour I sat on the bench where the Chief and I had talked so many times before. There were tears . . . and many fond memories. My mind was a blur, but a calm finally settled over me. I leaned over the rock wall and softly told the Chief *au revoir*. Someday we would meet again. Love survives.

That night at my brother's house in Roseburg I sat beneath a giant oak, one similar to the tree at Colliding Rivers. The clouds that afternoon had given the day a somber feel. But as night had fallen, the sky unexpectedly cleared. Between the branches of the tree I could see stars twinkling in the clear deep sky like precious jewels. It was quiet on Earth, but in heaven there was a celebration, of that I'm sure. A great Soul had returned.

I scribbled a few notes on the back of a napkin on the drive back to Portland the following morning. I wouldn't need them, however. I would always remember the day I said goodbye to my friend. And I would never forget "the night the oak trees wore diamonds."

*　　　*　　　*

"As one can see when the eyes are open,
so one can understand when the heart is open."
　　　　　　—Hazrat Inayat Khan,
　　　　　　1882–1927
　　　　　　Founder of the Sufi
　　　　　　Order of the West[4]

PART THREE

A Holographic View of the End Times

"Your vision will become clear only when you can look within your own heart.

Who looks outside, dreams; who looks inside, awakes."

—Carl Jung, 1875–1961
Founder of Analytical
Psychology[1]

–9–

Ho'oponopono

Five months after saying goodbye to the Chief I went to a lecture on water that changed my life. The date was August 15, 2001. I don't recall the speaker's name; in fact, he didn't even show up. A family emergency caused him to postpone the presentation.

When I arrived, a nondescript woman wearing a neatly pressed tan outfit was reading the note taped to the door. In the crowded hallway we struck up a casual conversation about the imprinting of water. She asked if I'd be interested in continuing our discussion in the book area, where interruptions would be minimal. It soon became apparent that the universe had arranged the cancellation of the lecture for my benefit.

Fariba

Once seated at a table, she introduced herself as Fariba. She had asked me to join her because she'd "sensed" that I was a spiritual seeker. [At a subsequent meeting I learned that she could read all of my *Akashic* records from other lifetimes.] Had I seen her from across a lecture hall, I would have given the middle-aged woman little notice.

At that time Fariba was living and working in a community a short distance from mine, perhaps ten minutes away. She'd come to America during the Shah's Revolution in Iran. Her English was polished, although her accent was thick when delivering certain words, like third. She pronounced it "terd."

Her "ice-breaking statement" set the tone for our three-hour conversation: "I've completely transcended the third dimension," she proclaimed matter-of-factly. I reached for my seat belt.

Generally when I'm around a spiritual person I get a feel for their aura, even though I can't actually see colors like some people. With Fariba this was different. Sitting across the table from her, my senses detected absolutely nothing. She told me that deer would walk right up to her in the woods when she was practicing her deep silence meditations.

Hailing from the same part of the world as Jalal al-Din Rumi and Shamus-i-Tabriz, I expected Fariba to be familiar with their work; but she acted like she had never heard their names. As a child she had talked to God. At an early age she'd learned to leave her physical body and travel through the worlds beyond. God had been her guide.

Fariba saw all of life as projected aspects of herself. This came from the realization that the outer world wasn't real. She would sweep her arms wide as we talked and exclaim, "This is all a joke. It's illusion. It isn't even real!" I had just finished writing *Dragon's Breath*; now the universe was giving me confirmation on its validity, as well as hints about my next endeavor, understanding the hologram.

Without indicating to her that I was a writer, she proceeded to verify much of the information the Chief had given me: a great shift was coming, huge changes in consciousness, lives would be turned upside down. When I asked about the December 21, 2012, date (still some years away) Fariba indicated that it was accurate, although the calendar could be off by as much as several months.

She had acquired self-knowledge that the world is but an illusion. One evening she had become one with the universe. She told me that she'd walked outside after meditating for several hours and discovered that she *was* the moon. From that point forward she *was* the sun, the stars, and everything outside of her.

Perhaps the most intriguing part of our first meeting was her description of the high worlds of Spirit. When speaking about these experiences, her intensity level ramped up. Her eyes turned into dancing pools of fiery light. She described being guided by God into regions where billions upon billions of colors exploded in space. There was a point amid these colors, a doorway, which led to an area where nothing existed, absolutely nothing. Fariba said there were no words in our vocabulary to describe it. Now, in her deep silence meditations, she returns to that region.

I sat spellbound for three hours as she described her life. She related that she always told the truth. Whenever someone asked her a question or spoke with her, she always gave them her full attention. She stayed until they were completely finished with the conversation. I noticed that, when listening to her, it was almost as if no "person" were present. As strange as it may sound, it felt like the Absolute was giving me information through this vehicle. It was both unnerving and transformational at the same time.

For Fariba, it was only the best in life. She dressed in fine clothes and drove an elegant white car. We met for coffee several times after that. But at no time during any of our lengthy discussions did I see her eat or drink anything. Out of respect for her, I never asked where she lived or worked. I only knew her as Fariba. I stopped calling because I sensed that she had more important things to do with her time than answer redundant questions of mine. She confided that she had an important mission, sometime in the future. I realized that she had given me all that I needed anyway—an inspirational push.

The day following our initial meeting I was scheduled to man a booth at the County Fair with a coworker. Our water district was handing out information and water samples. I was thankful for such light duty since I'd slept only a couple of hours. That day I was shown through waking dreams that my meeting with Fariba had been important.

To our delight, my coworker and I found that our booth overlooked an outdoor stage. One performer—a young woman who made and dressed in exotic bird costumes—captured our hearts. With tall stilts and bird-like antics, she entertained the crowd for most of our shift. Our favorite was her resplendent peacock outfit. For me, that specific eight-foot-tall bird was a powerful symbol of Awakening.

A second related incident happened that evening. An asphalt-covered walking trail circumscribed a field near my residence. There was one section, however, where only bare ground outlined the path. Often it was muddy, and traversing that section was difficult. I hadn't been out walking for a while, but this particular evening I decided to travel its entire length. To my surprise, when I reached the section of bare ground, I found that it was now covered with asphalt. An impression softly filtered into my consciousness: "The way is paved for you now."

Zero Limits

I have no doubt that the universe looks out for us. Key meetings such as the one with Fariba testify to that. Friends and mentors appear in our lives at just the right time. Books are no exception. On occasion, readers of my own books share the interesting ways they've come across them. I'm honored to have written something worth "finding."

From out of the blue, an employee from a bookstore in Virginia called one morning. The woman showered me with praise, thanking me for my contribution to their store. She told me they were sending customers out the door with two books; one was mine, and the second was a book by Joe Vitale and Dr. Ihaleakala Hew Len. I was touched that the woman would take the time to share this bit of news. Or was the universe behind this thoughtful gesture?

After hanging up the phone a light came on. What was that other book about, I wondered? A few minutes later I called the woman back and ordered a copy. *Zero Limits* arrived a week later and lit up my world! After reading the basic premise, I realized that I'd found the biggest piece yet to the holographic puzzle.

Vitale reveals a system used by Dr. Hew Len, who worked as a psychologist in the Hawaii State Hospital for three years. He was able to heal a ward of mentally ill patients without ever speaking with them. He never saw them professionally, nor did he counsel them. Dr. Len agreed to review their files, and when he did, he worked on himself. As he worked on himself, patients began to heal! He calls this system "Self-Identity *Ho'oponopono*," based on an ancient Hawaiian problem solving process.[2]

Mr. Redstone, the Chief, took full responsibility for his life. He would often pose the question, "How can we solve a problem that is not ours?" Dr. Len's Self-Identity *Ho'oponopono* took the Chief's philosophy of reflection to a whole new level. Dr. Len believed that he was 100 percent responsible for *everything* in his world. This included the struggles of his patients. He saw their problems as reflections of erroneous thoughts within himself. These he would transmute with love. This reinforced what the Chief had told me so often. When we create outside of love, we must one day take responsibility for our creations and balance them.

Had there been no connection between Dr. Len and the "outside world," this healing would not have occurred. I'm pretty sure Dr. Len knew the extent of this connection, but to speak of it openly could have cost him credibility. Vitale quipped that the 70-year-old healer was probably "a walking guru" to some; to others, "a nut case."[3] In the few instances I've shared my deeper insights on the hologram with friends, I noticed their eyes glazing over. One took a quick step back.

Dr. Len's success in healing the ward of mentally ill patients confirmed what I had never dared admit, either to myself or to others. The idea was simply too outlandish. Each person was living in a hologram of his or her own creation. That person was totally responsible for its creation and for its balancing—all of it. Furthermore, the hologram was made from that person's light. It essentially *was* that person!

Zero Limits reinforced the fact that we have an intimate connection with the universe. Dr. Len taught that we are responsible for everything in our life simply because *it is in our life.* "In a literal sense," he stated, "the entire world is our creation." According to Dr. Len, everything we encounter that we don't like—terrorism, politics, commercialism, environmental destruction, etc.—is up to us to heal. He said flatly, "They don't exist, in a manner of speaking, except as projections from inside us."[4]

Carl Jung once predicted that a Hitler-type personality would emerge on the world stage after studying the psyche of the people. This would represent the shadow side of the group consciousness, currently in denial. When we encounter darkness in our world, we are actually meeting reflections of our shadow that we need to heal. We shirk our responsibility, however, due to a lack of understanding.

I've found that spiritual organizations in general are notorious for being dysfunctional. Whereas before I would complain about their use of fear and commercialism to expand memberships and control their followers, after contemplating on Dr. Len's approach, I began to view these abuses as reflections of the group consciousness; specifically, I began to see the individuals within that group's dysfunctional shadow side. Rather than being something to criticize, I now looked upon

139

these flaws as opportunities to heal erroneous thoughts within myself. Remember, our responsibility extends to everything in our lives.

[I once asked the Chief what kept us tied to the Seedbed and our problems. The answer I expected was "fear," but his response was a resounding "lack of self-responsibility."]

The Chief's Golden Formula is a method of transmuting the Seedbed with self-responsibility, imagination, and wisdom. (Wisdom has a higher vibrational frequency than the contents of our Seedbed.) *Ho'oponopono* does the same thing, only with love. Healing involves loving ourselves, *all* of ourselves. This encompasses aspects currently in denial, including the shadow.

Dr. Len talked about returning to the "zero state." Mr. Redstone called this return to stillness, "zero point," or, "the fulcrum of the light wave." The still point in the center of each and every light wave is the non-polarity, Divine state of being. The simple formula Dr. Len used to clean and polish his world is as follows: "I love you, I'm sorry, please forgive me, thank you." That's it.

In his therapeutic work, Dr. Len prefaced the formula by asking Source, or Divine Love, to correct any erroneous thoughts, first in himself, and then in his client.[5] By doing this, a link was made to the higher frequencies that would do the work of transmuting the Seedbed. It was a given that he had already taken full responsibility for everything in his world. In finishing, Dr. Len would turn the problem over to Divine Spirit and ask that it be released. The similarities to the Chief's Golden Formula were astounding. [A *Ho'oponopono* version of the Golden Formula appears at the end of this chapter. The original Golden Formula can be found in *Dragon's Breath* on page 91.]

When I began integrating *Ho'oponopono* into the Golden Formula, I found myself saying, "I love you, I'm sorry (for creating this problem outside of love), please forgive me, thank you (for balancing the energy to zero point.") Whether this is the way others might practice it, I cannot say. To each according to his own understanding.

Preparing the Room

When I was trying to get comfortable speaking in front of people, I found it helpful to arrive early and "get acquainted" with the room. It made me feel more at ease while giving the talk. I would sit with the room for a few minutes and let my energy spread out and "soften" it. That's how it felt. But as it turns out, I was also letting the room get acquainted with me.

Dr. Len, who is keenly aware of energies, had his own method of preparing a room. Before asking permission to enter, he would ask the room its name.[6] He believed that every room had a name, as well as other so-called inanimate objects. If the room told him "No, it's not okay to enter," Dr. Len would then use his simple formula to "clean" his consciousness. Once allowed inside, he would ask how the curtains were, for example, and then the tables, chairs, and so on.

A chair might complain about the last person who sat on it. Perhaps the occupant had left thoughts of despair and hopelessness upon it. Dr. Len would see this problem as an issue to clean, a common problem that he and the chair both shared. He would constantly clean his surroundings, thereby balancing erroneous thoughts and returning them to zero, the state of the Divine.

Dr. Len was extremely conscious of his thoughts and words. He would never, for instance, complain about the water he was drinking by saying, "This is bad." By calling it bad, he would imbue the water with those vibrations and his body would receive it as such. In Japan, Dr. Masaru Emoto's revolutionary work proved that thought influences the physical make up of water.

In one memorable case, Dr. Emoto took water crystal photos of polluted Lake Biwa.[7] Dark and deformed crystals reflected the harsh consciousness of those who had frequented the area. Thoughts of love and gratitude were then directed into the water on several occasions by a group of Dr. Emoto's followers. A subsequent photo revealed beautiful, six-sided crystals that now radiated much more light.

The same principle applies to food. The way we think about food affects its quality and influences how the body receives it. Have you ever noticed how commercials "program our minds" to believe a product has a curative or beautifying value? As we believe, so shall we receive. Those who fully understand this principle bless their food with love and gratitude before each meal.

A Touch of Irony

I found it difficult reading *Zero Limits*. Yes, the font was a bit small, and the light-gray ink could have been a little darker. But I could live with these questionable publishing decisions. The reason I nearly put the book down on several occasions? Joe Vitale's blatant self-promotion.

While Dr. Len's contributions were well worth the price of the book, the self-promotion by Vitale put me off. His focus on using spiritual tools for manifesting wealth seemed more important to him than Soul's growth and awakening. This added to my chagrin. But upon reflection, I found myself thanking him as much for these irritants as for writing the book!

I had already learned about the mechanics of reflection from talks with the Chief. Dr. Len's *Ho'oponopono* reinforced my intent to take full responsibility for my life, even these bothersome reflections that I pinned on others. Dr. Len would playfully ask, "Have you ever noticed that whenever you have a problem, you are there?"[8]

I realized that my Higher Self was directing my attention to the next thing I needed to clean—self-promotion. At one of our first meetings, the Chief had shared an important insight that bears repeating: "Whatever is currently giving us physical discomfort, mental anguish, or emotional pain, that will be the next thing we need to clear."

Yes, I was definitely feeling mental anguish! Joe Vitale was kind enough to scrape his fingernails across the blackboard for my benefit. Providing I was aware enough, I would find the jewel hidden in this "tattered, self-promotional box." And I did. By combining my understanding of *Ho'oponopono* with the Chief's Golden Formula, I came up with a tool for accessing the treasure (found at the end of this chapter).

In truth, self-promotion wasn't *his* problem. It was mine. Joe was only the messenger. Others may have benefited greatly from his allusion to the other books and articles he'd written. No doubt some had purchased the book strictly to secure wealth, health, peace, and more. I was simply interested in the "more" part—Awakening.

One with the Universe

After listening to the Chief for over three years, studying various spiritual philosophies, and reading about *Ho'oponopono,* I still had some doubts about my expanded view of the world. After all, believing that the universe was an extension of my light was pretty unbelievable. It took an unexpected revelation to drive this realization home.

Immediately following my short introduction to *Ho'-oponopono,* the hologram occupied much of my attention. One sunny afternoon I was driving through the Oregon countryside enjoying a clear view of Mt. Hood with its snow-laden summit. Without conscious effort or intention, I suddenly found myself in an altered state of consciousness. One minute I was the driver of a swiftly moving vehicle, enjoying the greenery of spring, the next I had become everything in my universe. Simply everything!

There was nothing that was not made from my light. I gazed out in awe upon the fields and pastures I had driven by countless times. There were cows and horses, fences and barns. They were my light. And the roadway with its approaching cars—also my light. Above me soared sparrows and hawks, blackbirds, and doves. I was the wind that carried them and the mountain that inspired them. All things big and small were clothed in my light.

My consciousness touched all that surrounded me. For several minutes I was no-thing, yet everything. My driving was not affected; a part of me was left in charge of the mundane.

With this realization came only knowingness. It was stark, still, unassuming, colorless, odorless. There was joy, but not the joy of "having" or "doing." It was the sheer joy of pure realization, pure being. It was calm, peaceful, serene, free. Those were the adjectives that seemed to apply. Perhaps this realization would have been more profound accompanied by flutes and violins. I do not know. The silence was remarkable in its own right. I'd experienced ecstasy and joy with other altered states, but this was surprisingly different; it simply *was*. While it was not an "end-all" experience, it brought home the realization that my theory about the hologram was correct. I knew!

Without the gift of this experience I would never have written this book. The universe must have known that. Upon reflection, I compared my experience to a theater projector. Rather than looking at the images on the screen, my attention was focused on the light filtering through the dimly lit theater. The light carried with it images that would become people, places, and events in the movie. This may not be the best analogy, but it's the closest to the actual experience I can come up with at the moment.

Words do their best to convey meaning, but true meaning is reserved for realization. The highest realization is that we are loved beyond measure; in fact, we are love, itself. *Ho'oponopono* and the Golden Formula give us powerful tools for cleaning out the Seedbed. With each chorus of "I love you" we move closer to the heart . . . but it takes effort on our part.

*   *   *

"When your soul experiences memories (replaying as problems), say to them mentally or silently: 'I love you dear memories. I am grateful for the opportunity to free all of you and me.'"

—Dr. Ihaleakala Hew Len
"Who's In Charge?"
(2005)[9]

HO'OPONOPONO GOLDEN FORMULA
for Eliminating Problems, Fears, and Addictions

Connect with the Divine

In the name of my I AM Presence I call upon Divine Spirit (or my Higher Self) to help balance this problem.

Imagination

Use the imagination to put the problem into picture form. This bypasses the sensory mind and Belief System. You should also include yourself in the picture (and your spiritual guide if you choose). We are simply holding the attention on the problem, not trying to solve it. It doesn't have to be an accurate representation. Take your time. Acknowledge, feel, and release any emotional pain that comes up. Do this without judgment.

Understanding

I understand that the universe is my creation and therefore my responsibility.

I understand that I've created this problem outside of love.

I understand that the problem is within me; I am not trying to change or heal the outer reflection.

Balance and Release

I love you, I'm sorry, please forgive me, thank you.

I love you, I'm sorry, please forgive me, thank you.

I love you, I'm sorry, please forgive me, thank you.

I hereby release the problem and call upon my Higher Self to transmute my Seedbed. So Be It.

–10–

Mt. Shasta and Inner Earth

In the late 1980s I heard a story—it could have been from the Chief—that stuck in my mind. A group of media executives were invited to Los Angeles for a preview of emerging technologies. As I recall, a man wearing a business suit came out on stage and proceeded to speak about holograms and their future use in communication and entertainment. Military applications were also mentioned.

At one point the presenter walked off the stage and meandered down two different aisleways amid the seated attendees. As the presentation neared its conclusion, with all eyes fixed on the lecturer, he drove home his closing point. He simply disappeared. He'd been a holographic image!

The Mother Paradox

Of course the audience had been interacting with holograms well before that presentation in Los Angeles. They had just called them something else—friend, brother, father, mother. In truth, everyone we meet is a cosmic hologram. Once I finally came to this realization, the answer to a very intriguing question, one that had haunted me for years, became apparent. The question was this: If my mother died when I was young and later reincarnated as my great niece, then at the time of my passing how could that Soul welcome me to the land beyond as my mother?

The answer came to me while I was writing the Introduction to this book. Reality exists exclusively in the worlds *beyond* duality. What we experience in our everyday lives are reflections of reality encased in cube-shaped vacuum chambers. The universe we are currently experiencing is a 3-D hologram, a projection. We interpret the frequency fields as the third dimension because our consciousness is stationed on the plane above it. When you think about it, our image appears in many places at once, in the holograms of all our friends and loved ones simultaneously.

The Soul that played the role of my mother in this life agreed to send a likeness of herself into my theater. That likeness will also appear in a later scene when I'm leaving this world. She has agreed to meet me at the time of my passing in the form I will recognize, as she appeared as my mom. That loving Soul who played the part of my mother has also signed on to an additional role, that of my great niece (speculation). A different likeness will be called for, but well within that Soul's abilities to manifest.

We underestimate the magnificence of ourselves as Soul. We are vast, cosmic beings. In fact, we are appearing in a multitude of roles throughout time simultaneously. Past and future exist together in the "cosmic now." Time is but an illusion. Those who consciously access "reality" can project their image wherever and whenever they choose. We call these Souls "Masters."

"Auld Lang Syne" and Mt. Shasta

Just as there is a connection between "Joy to the World" and Colliding Rivers, there is also an obscure link between "Auld Lang Syne" and Mt. Shasta. The famous Robert Burns poem, "Auld Lang Syne," was written in 1788 and later paired with a popular folk song, "Roud #6294." The lyrics vary because they were collected from an ancient oral tradition by Burns and others, a memorial passed down orally since the "olden times."[1]

Although it can herald a beginning, traditionally the song symbolizes endings. "Auld Lang Syne" is most commonly played on New Year's Eve each year. The song's Scots title is sometimes translated into English as "long long ago." It had never been put into print until Burns took down the words from a very old man.

While growing up, for no apparent reason, tears would well up in my eyes whenever I heard "Auld Lang Syne." A melancholy, heaviness of heart would accompany it. The first threads of this mystery began to unravel when I was twenty-one, en route from southern Oregon to San Francisco to attend a metaphysical event.

Late morning I passed the City of Mt. Shasta exit on Interstate 5 on a clear fall day. The 14,179-foot peak, located about 10 miles away, rose majestically from the valley floor on my left. The most unusual sensation came over me when I gazed up at the snow-capped peak. A very powerful and seemingly important memory began to surface; its origin lay hidden just below the threshold of consciousness. Unfortunately, I could never grasp the subtle thread.

With each subsequent visit to California I would attempt to access the memory. It never happened. Many years later, however, I came across a story that solved the mystery in impressive fashion. That's when I discovered the fascinating link between "Auld Lang Syne" and my enchanting mountain, Mt. Shasta.[2]

The Backstory

California was once part of the Lemurian continent, sometimes referred to as "the Motherland." According to the Naacal writings, reported to be the first written records of man, its 64,000,000 inhabitants developed one of the greatest civilizations known to earth. Initially called "MU," Lemuria colonized much of the ancient world prior to its final destruction about 12,000 years ago.[3] The continent predated Atlantis, whose controlling agenda directed towards lesser-evolved cultures was in opposition to that of the peaceful, non-interfering Lemurians.

About 25,000 years ago a series of thermonuclear wars over ideologies weakened the structures of both continents. The Lemurian priests realized that their beloved Motherland would perish beneath the waves of the Pacific in less than 15,000 years. (A lifespan of 20,000 to 30,000 years was common for the inhabitants of Lemuria.)

A very large cavern existed beneath Mt. Shasta. The Lemurian priesthood petitioned Shamballa-the-Lesser, the governing body of the Inner Earth network of cities called Agartha (sometimes spelled Agharta). They requested permission to expand the dome within the mountain and build a city to preserve both their culture and their records.[4]

Before permission was granted, the Lemurians were asked to prove that they had learned the lessons of peace, both to the Agarthans and to galactic agencies such as the Galactic Confederation of Planets. The original Lemurians had come from the stars, places like Sirius B, Alpha Centauri, and many lesser-known planets.

It was recognized that this part of California would survive the coming cataclysm. This region of Lemuria, called Telos, extended from what we know today as the southwestern United States upwards into British Columbia.[5] The Lemurians constructed their city to hold approximately 200,000 people. They named it Telos, after that region.

Unfortunately, only 25,000 people made it safely to the sanctuary when the destruction came earlier than anticipated. During the night, while the masses slept, under a starry blue sky, the continent of Lemuria slipped quietly beneath the waters of the Pacific. There had been no unusual weather patterns during the day to forewarn of disaster. Their beloved Motherland went down overnight!

Just prior to the sinking, many of the priests and priestesses returned from Telos to their homes on the continent to be with their countrymen. They returned to counter the fear that always accompanies a cataclysmic event. Every deep trauma leaves scars upon the etheric body, taking lifetimes to heal. Using spiritual energies, these priests and priestesses wrapped the auras of the people in a blanket of peace. This created a shield so their etheric bodies would not be so severely scarred. This saved the inhabitants of the Motherland from having to experience greater tragedy in future embodiments.

Many members of the priesthood placed themselves in small groups in strategic locations throughout the continent. They sang and prayed as the Motherland eased down into the water. The melody of the song heard that night is known today as "Auld Lang Syne." At last I know why it means so much to me—the song is a tribute to those who lost their lives during the sinking of Lemuria.

When the priests and priestesses sacrificed their own lives to stay with their people, much fear was mitigated and a certain level of harmony was maintained. The damage to those Souls that perished was greatly reduced. It was said that the priesthood and musicians sang and prayed until the water reached the level of their mouths. None left their post or succumbed to fear. Lemuria went down with dignity. "Auld Lang Syne" was the last song ever heard on the beloved Motherland.

Although the memories lie buried, those present on Lemuria during that tragic, yet peaceful, night are still moved when they hear the song from "long long ago." It was prophesied before the cataclysm that one day, in some distant future, many of those who sacrificed their lives would gather together and sing "Auld Lang Syne" again. A reunion would take place between the surface dwellers and their fifth dimensional brothers whose ancestors live today beneath Mt. Shasta.[6]

Telos

My first introduction to the subterranean city of Telos came from a book called, *A Dweller on Two Planets*, published in 1952.[7] The author, Phylos, tells of a secret doorway hidden behind a solid rock cliff. The passage leads into the mountain, where an advanced race of beings lives in peace. Many visitors to Panther Meadow on Mt. Shasta tell of encounters with tall, youthful beings with great wisdom. The secret doorway leading inside the mountain is likely hidden nearby. On occasion, people have even been given access to the underground city.

Dianne Robbins and Aurelia Louise Jones have written and spoken extensively on both Telos and the Agarthan network of subterranean cities. Some interesting facts about the "modern-day Lemurians" and the Inner Earth civilizations follow.

According to a spokesperson from within Telos, the top of the interior dome is situated on a level even with the midway point of the mountain. The bottom of the dome is about even with the mountain's base. The deepest levels of the city extend nearly a mile below ground. Five levels comprise the city of approximately 1.5 million people:[8] (Level one is the uppermost.)

Level 1: (Main level) Public buildings and living areas

Level 2: Manufacturing, classes, living space

Level 3: Hydroponic gardens

Level 4: Half devoted to gardens, the rest for manufacturing and nature

Level 5: Nature level with lakes, parks, and wildlife

Residents of Telos have been vegetarians for over 12,000 years. Their diet consists largely of vegetables, fruits, grains, and nuts. No meat is eaten, and no life is taken. Fear creates aggression. Over the course of time, the aggressive qualities of the citizens of Telos and their animals have dropped away. On the nature level, one would be shocked to find "predatory animals" nibbling on grasses and leaves. Animals and plants, long extinct on the surface, may still be found in Telos. This includes the dodo bird, wooly mammoth, and saber-toothed tiger.[9]

Water in Telos is crystal clear, unpolluted, and "alive." It contains a "conscious vitality" unknown to surface dwellers. Water in Telos speaks telepathically to those who swim in it. Temperature is adjusted to the swimmer's desire. Telosians say that the water on the surface has lost its voice.[10] Plants in both the natural areas and hydroponic gardens convert carbon monoxide to oxygen. Vents to the surface have been closed off due to the pollution now suffocating the cities above ground.[11]

No monetary system is used in Telos. All necessities of life are provided free of charge. A barter system allows for the exchange of artwork, massages, and other such luxuries. The inhabitants choose how they would like to contribute to society. One might work in the hydroponic gardens for four hours a day, for example. Another might design and manufacture clothing. Menial jobs such as cleaning up after animals in parks and collecting and dematerializing garbage are shared equally by all in turn. Community service is looked upon as an honor, rather than drudgery to be avoided.

The temple, located in the center of the main level of Telos, was designed to hold 10,000 people. The crystal capstone of the pyramid-shaped building came from Venus. It is infused with light. They call the material "livingstone." The capstone turns different colors on different days, reflecting the predominant color-ray pouring into our planet from the sun at varying times of the week. On Tuesday, for example, the livingstone is blue. Sensitive negotiations are carried out on this day. On yellow-ray days, the Telosians build intellect. Pink-ray days are best for artistic endeavors. The temple is run by the Melchizedek Priesthood, an order existing everywhere in the universe.[12]

A group known as the Council of Twelve oversees the administrative duties and makes important decisions pertaining to the city. Six men and six women provide balance to the council. Smaller groups of twelve oversee affairs at the community level. Arbitrators are called upon to settle disputes, generally at the onset of any problem. Members of the priesthood are chosen for these roles. They are able to access the Akashic records of the individuals involved, and their decisions are never questioned.

Even though Telosians have essentially the same biological makeup as we do, their lifespans are incredibly long. We believe that growing old and dying after sixty to eighty years is a given.[13] Our Inner Earth brothers and sisters have no destructive beliefs limiting their lifespan. They live as long as they choose. There are individuals living in Telos who survived the cataclysm more than 12,000 years ago.[14]

After living in the same body for the time of their choosing, a Telosian simply lays it aside or ascends with it, depending upon the needs of Soul. The dimensional shift on the horizon for many on the surface would be no big deal to a resident of Telos. From an early age, Telosians are taught spiritual practices and disciplines that make their lives abundant, fun, productive, and free of fear.

Perhaps the most astounding and enviable facet of Telosian life revolves around their computer system. Organic, "living" computers pick up communications from across the galaxy. They can also display past lives in detail, coordinate transportation systems, and monitor and diagnose health issues with pinpoint accuracy. These advanced computers are connected to the "Christ Mind." They cannot be used for negativity or harmful intent. The Telosian computer system connects with other cities in Agartha, as well as compatible systems throughout our galaxy.[15]

Holodecks, similar to the one portrayed in "Star Trek," function much like our film studios. Telosians create programs to be enjoyed either interactively, or viewed as observers. Since Earth is a school for learning "conscious creation," many forms of creativity are sponsored in Telos.

Light in Telos comes from two primary sources. The sun is a crystal that was brought to Telos from another planet. It will burn for approximately one million years. Full spectrum light nourishes both physical bodies and the hydroponic gardens. Telosians also have an advanced technology that can charge stone with artificial light. The objects become small "suns" that burn for half a million years. Walls and tunnels radiate a soft glow from using this technology.

Advanced boring machines carve tunnels that are both watertight and diamond-hard. They have a built-in elasticity, which makes them earthquake proof. Their "tube system" connects Telos with a sister city in Lassen, as well as other subterranean civilizations in Agartha. High speed electromagnetic trains reach speeds of 3,000 miles per hour, never touching the walls of the tubes.[16]

A shuttle system services Telos with crystalline "floating baskets" controlled by the mind of the rider.

Computers act as traffic controllers, intervening when potential collisions are detected. By misusing the baskets, a Telosian can lose his or her traveling rights for brief periods of time. Reckless driving is seldom a problem in Telos, however, as their citizens are much more responsible than surface drivers.

The Sinking of Atlantis

The nuclear exchanges during the Lemurian-Atlantean War left pockets of devastation upon the surface world that remain to this day—the Sahara, the Gobi, the Australian Outback. Atlantis survived approximately two hundred years beyond the disappearance of Lemuria. "Survived" is the key word here.

Earthquakes measuring 15 points on the Richter Scale rocked the Earth when Lemuria went under. Huge tidal waves swept inland hundreds of miles, destroying everything in their path. By today's geography, the walls of water would have stretched from Los Angeles, California as far east as Oklahoma City, Oklahoma.[17]

When survivors tried to rebuild their cities, tremors would reward their efforts with more destruction. People fled the cities for the safety of rural lands. The Great Pyramid was one of the few structures that survived the cataclysm, since it had been built with divine mathematical proportions.

The Atlantean priests spearheaded the construction of a city of their own. Beneath the region now known as Mato Grosso in Brazil, they were given permission to build their subterranean city, Posid. The Atlanteans were able to save their priceless records, too. They selected their brightest minds to survive the cataclysm

157

and resurrect their civilization from within the Earth. They also had to prove to the Agarthan Councils and Confederation of Planets that they had learned the lessons from their previous actions.[18]

Agartha

The Inner Earth Network of Agartha consists of 120 cities with a total population of approximately 25 million people.[19] Some came to Earth at the request of Heavenly Councils to oversee the planet. Many others arrived over a million years ago from another solar system when the great Galactic Wars were raging throughout the galaxy. Inner Earth afforded them safety from marauding bands of roving ETs.

Some Agarthan civilizations have been living inside the Earth for *millions* of years! These advanced beings recognized that Earth was the showcase of the Milky Way Galaxy due to its diverse variety of mineral, plant, and animal life. They saw our planet as a "living library." Aside from the residents of Telos and Posid, Hollow Earth beings have never resided on the surface.[20]

Many years ago I read about secret tunnels hidden beneath the Potala Monastery in Lhasa, Tibet. These reportedly led to Inner Earth, where secret archives and archeological treasures were hidden. Telepathic lamas guarded these tunnels. T. Lobsang Rampa penned *The Third Eye* and *The Cave of the Ancients*. He wrote of following his guide into these tunnels where he was shown ancient manuscripts and the skeletons of giants.

Shamballa is the governing city of Agartha. It is located in the very heart of the planet, and can be accessed through either the North or South Pole. The northern and southern lights are reflections from Inner Earth's Central Sun.[21]

Earth's crust is approximately 800 miles from the outer to the inner surface. Because our planet is hollow, as are all planets, the center of gravity is not in the center; it is in the center of its crust, 400 miles below the surface. The source of Earth's magnetic field has been a mystery. The Inner Sun is the actual power behind our magnetic field.

In the 1930s all tunnels and passages leading to Agartha were closed off by Inner Earth civilizations. The two main entries, the North and South Pole, were closed in the year 2000. Magnetic force fields were installed to prevent intrusion by rogue governments on the surface. At one time several tunnels led directly to the Inner Earth Library in Catharia, a sister city of Telos located beneath the Aegean Sea. One such tunnel was located beneath the Library of Alexandria. These entrances have been closed, as well.[22]

Library of Porthologos

The Library of Porthologos in Catharia spans 456 square miles, and houses crystal slides containing the entire history of our universe.[23] They are living records, playing out their roles as holographic scenes. There are mini-theaters spread throughout the library. Visitors can watch any event in history come alive before their very eyes.[24]

The outer grounds of Porthologos feature manicured lawns, colorful flowers, musical fountains, and energizing waterfalls. The water is alive and fully conscious. It sings. Melodies of peace and love harmonize and heal every cell in the body.

Inside the library is a crystal staircase that leads to a door that opens up into the universe. You are surrounded in space by the Milky Way Galaxy; you feel a part of All That Is. Porthologos is a multi-dimensional portal. You can travel anywhere in the universe by your thoughts and intentions.[25]

The chairs in the gardens and alcoves call to you. When you sit down, you are instantly connected with the "internal library computer system." The knowledge of the universe is there at your fingertips. No library cards are necessary. Your identification is inscribed in your DNA.[26]

The Chief also called Earth a "living library." He was aware of how diverse and precious our planet really is. While he had mentioned the city beneath Mt. Shasta more than once, I never pressed him for many details. Looking back, there are many avenues of thought that we left unexplored. But the Chief did inspire me to dream, and for that I'm most thankful.

*　　　　　*　　　　　*

"All we dream we create, and all we create, we honor."
—Adama
High Priest of Telos[27]

–11–

Event Horizon: Zero Point

If you told your friends that you were the center of the universe, they might think you were a bit egotistical and eccentric, but you'd be right. Of course, they could say the same thing. Indeed, every point is the center of the universe.

Think of your favorite movie. Now, imagine filming that movie from not one camera angle, but from every possible camera angle. The movie could be viewed through the eyes of any one of the actors. Each character would appear to be the center of the action. More or less, this is what we are doing right now. We are all stars of our own "Lifetime Original Movie."

The Center of the World

While standing on Harney Peak in the Black Hills, an Oglala Sioux medicine man named Black Elk witnessed a vision. He saw the spirit of all things interconnected, living together as one being. While in that altered state, he made the seemingly outlandish claim that Harney Peak was the center of the world. In reality, he was experiencing his own holographic projection. It was not Harney Peak that was the center; Black Elk himself was the center. As Black Elk later put it, "Anywhere is the center of the world."[1]

We hear the term "singularity" more and more these days. In the center of each sentient being in the universe can be found a single point, a singularity. It lies in the heart of man. From this still point, everything we experience in our outer world radiates. To this still point, the zero point, everything returns. This expression of ideas, and their subsequent return to stillness, is happening all the time.

As the Chief explained, the principles of radiation and contraction enable this cosmic motion picture to take place. From the Realm of Stillness and Unity, the Absolute begins with a single point. A line is drawn in both directions from the center. Each point on the line then moves outward, forming a plane in the shape of a square. A second dimension is born.

To achieve a third dimension, each point on the flat plane must move upward at the same rate. This forms the boundary within which the reflection of creation is manifested. The cube is the basic building block of the material world. A polarity shaft runs vertically through the center of the cube. In the middle is the fulcrum, or zero point.

> "In My universe there is but one form
> from which all forms appear. That one form
> is the pulsing cube-sphere, two halves of the
> heartbeat of My dual thinking."
> —Walter Russell,
> from *The Secret of Light* [2]

Our individual universe is a holographic movie playing continuously in these cube-shaped vacuum chambers (light waves). Other platonic solids, representing planes of consciousness beyond our own, fit nicely into the cube. Ideas in the form of frequencies are sent forth from the fulcrum in the center of the light wave. These "frames" in our cosmic film flash through the projector of our consciousness at billions of times per second. Still images appear to be in motion. We experience these frequencies as "our world," once the brain does its magic of converting them into objective reality.[3]

We are actually picture-making machines. Without us the universe would not exist. We are its creators. We can now answer the age-old question: If a tree falls in the forest and no one hears it, did it really fall? No, because no one was around to create it.

When the frequencies return to stillness, they don't return with the exact same information that they left with. They return enhanced, due to our interactions with them, our lessons, our discoveries, and our observations. This is how Stillness, or the One Reality, benefits from dividing Itself into many in order to experience the hologram.

Nassim Haremein, a prominent young physicist, reinforced Black Elk's discovery. His work confirms the existence of the hologram. Haremein states that each person is the center of his or her own universe.[4] He points out that the current Big Bang Theory is only partially correct. Yes, of course the universe is expanding; it's in the expressive phase. But once the Outbreath of creation is complete, it will experience a contraction toward its center, the Inbreath. According to Haremein, every point in the universe has a black hole at its center. This is the singular point where Divinity steps out of Unity and into Duality.

163

Haremein, David Wilcock, and Drunvalo Melchizedek, among others, all refer to the double toroid shape of our universe (Fig. 1). It's fascinating how the double torus shape within a light wave takes on the configuration of a *vesica piscus*, that of two overlapping circles. In Figure 1, the upper sphere represents the universe we occupy. It flows into our parallel universe, what Stuart Wilde calls our "Mirror World,"[5] the bottom sphere. Universes are born in pairs, shared jointly by each "complementary half." This raises interesting questions: Is there a complementary Earth, as well? Do I have a twin that has been totally unaware of me? If so, is he reading about the Mirror World right now and pondering these same questions?

According to Drunvalo, there is a small space within the human heart—perhaps what the Chief has called "the fifth chamber"—from which our universe flows. From this creative fulcrum, two torroidal fields form around our body approximately 8 to 10 feet in diameter. Incredibly, this tiny singularity within our heart is the source of the entire universe that we experience![6]

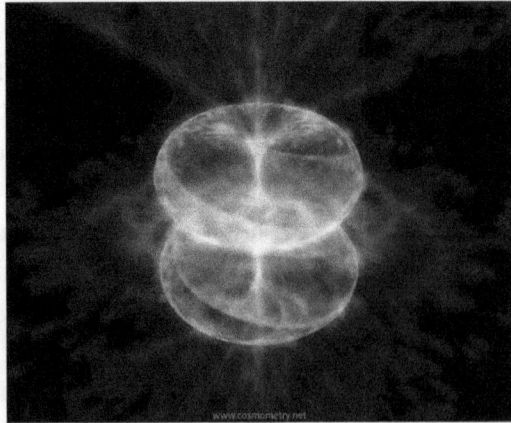

Figure 1: Double Torus from cosmometry.net[7]

Cycles

When I first heard the Chief talk about light waves, I imagined an hourglass situated in the center of a cube. In my mind I would watch the last grains of sand fall into the center point, then disappear into the chamber below. I would then flip the hourglass over and see the bottom, now the top, repeat the process. It didn't occur to me at the time that I was witnessing cycles.

The expression half of the creative process represents one half of the cycle; the voidance half completes it. It takes 26,000 years for our solar system to circle our Central Sun, Alcyone. This tells us that the Outbreath for this large light wave is 13,000-years long. At the end of 2012 we will have reached the completion of the Outbreath. An equal duration is reserved for the Inbreath.

The significance of the ending of the Mayan Calendar has not gone unnoticed. Many point to December 21, 2012, as a time of great change. The excitement and awe surrounding this date is further heightened by the synchronous ending of four major cycles.

With our entrance into Aquarius, the 2,160-year cycle of the Piscean Age is coming to a close. At the same time, Earth's 26,000-year Precession of the Equinoxes—a Mayan Great Cycle—finds completion. Furthermore, according to both the Aztec and Mayan cosmologies, 2012 is the end-point of a 104,000-year cycle composed of four Great Cycles. But most astounding of all is the completion of our solar system's 225-million-year Galactic Orbit, also slated for 2012.[8]

Event Horizons

Imagine a swinging pendulum. As it reaches its outermost point on its journey to the right, it must pause

165

before it begins the return. Once again, when it swings to the widest point left, it must pause. Our breathing mirrors this behavior. We breathe in, pause, exhale, and then pause again before breathing in. Light waves are the prototype for this action. Each pause is, in fact, a zero point.

Ideas radiate out until they reach their full expression near the boundary of the cube where they encounter inert gasses. Creation reaches an end point. This is the first event horizon. According to the Chief, the cube-shaped light wave then turns inside out to maintain a northerly direction. The journey back to zero point in the center begins. Then, at this end-point of creation, the second event horizon is encountered.

Timelines converge as they spiral in to an event horizon. Just as sand in an hourglass falls into its center point, events in our lives are carried forward; only timelines follow spiral patterns as they approach the event horizon. As we spiral into the fulcrum, time, as we experience it, will speed up.

Terrance and Dennis McKenna, two scientists from the United States, believe that the universe is a hologram made up of 64 waves, or time scales. The number 64 shows up in several interesting places: the number of codons in our DNA, the number of hexagrams in the I-Ching, and the number of keys to the Tree of Life. The McKenna's computer modeling suggests that all 64 waves of time will peak together in 2012.

The McKennas point out that changes in consciousness are following the pattern of time waves. Tighter and tighter spirals will result in even greater leaps in consciousness. Their data predicts that in a period of 384 days, as we approach the end of the Mayan

Calendar, there will be more transformations of consciousness than in all the previous cycles put together. As we approach the winter equinox, there will be a six-day cycle in which events will move even faster. In the final 135 minutes there will be eighteen further enormous leaps in consciousness.[9]

At Zero Point

But what will we experience at the moment we reach zero point? One current scientific view contends that "an observer crossing a black hole event horizon can calculate the moment they've crossed it, but will not actually see or feel anything special happen at that moment."[10]

Mr. Redstone believed that we would experience Unity Consciousness, if only temporarily, when we reached zero point. The forces that normally weigh us down would be lifted. At this time we could commune directly with our Higher Self. In those moments, hours, or days, we would experience the joy and ecstasy that is our natural, divine state.

Andrew Basiago claimed that some participants in Project Pegasus, who were sent forward in time to the end of 2012, reported that they had experienced perfect bliss upon reaching zero point. Others described a sheet of white light. Beyond December 21, 2012, they could see absolutely nothing.[11]

Saul, writing through John Smallman, a Reconnective Healer, claims that humanity is nearing the endpoint of a dream that got out of control. Originally we sought to experience what it would be like to be separate from God, to create from the viewpoint of limited beings. But later we got lost in Dreamland and forgot

167

that we were dreaming. A horrific nightmare ensued. But humanity is now stirring from its brief, but intense, nap.

According to Smallman, the moment of our awakening into Reality is at hand. He writes: "Be prepared for mighty life-altering events to happen and appear before you as you awaken at last into Reality. . . ."[12]

The End of Time Window

On October 24, 2007, both the Maya and the Hopi Nations declared that the fabled Blue Star Kachina had arrived. Two hundred years earlier, the Hopi had prophesied that a blue star would appear to herald a shift in our evolution. When Comet Holmes entered our solar system and subsequently exploded, a blue sphere emerged and immediately began to expand. In less than 24 hours, the 17th magnitude comet brightened by a factor of nearly a million. It grew larger and larger, and by mid-November it had eclipsed the diameter of the sun. It was the largest object ever to be seen in our solar system.[13]

This important declaration by the Maya and Hopi in the fall of 2007, triggered by the explosion of Comet Holmes, signaled the beginning of the End of Time. Drunvalo Melchizedek, a spokesperson for many Indigenous tribes, states that the Maya believe that a Seven-Year Window opened up on October 24, 2007. Somewhere within that window monumental changes in both the world and our consciousness will occur. That it will happen exactly on the end-date of the Mayan Calendar—December 21, 2012—is extremely unlikely.[14]

But on that end-date a ceremony will be performed by the Maya to conclude a 13,000-year cycle. The following day an even more important event will take place: a ceremony celebrating the beginning of the next cycle. Polarity will shift on this planet from the masculine to the feminine. For the next 13,000 years, women will hold the power positions on the planet.[15]

According to Hopi prophecy, a red star will appear to signal the closing of the End of Time Window. This is projected to happen between November and December of 2015. While this could happen up to a year earlier, Drunvalo states that the window will definitely close before January 1, 2016. He also offers one possibility for the red star's appearance. Betelgeuse is one of four stars that frame Orion's Belt. It is currently imploding. Drunvalo believes that Betelgeuse could become a supernova and turn into a red giant.[16]

All Things Revealed

A Mayan prophecy states that in 2010 all of their knowledge would start to come back to them. Until recently, only three Mayan Codices were in circulation. All the rest had been hidden from the Spanish conquistadors and their locations were unknown. By 2012, the prophecy continues, *all* of the Mayan knowledge would return.

In 2011 one thousand Codices were found in the basement of a museum in Los Angeles. So far, all efforts to get them released have failed. The elite don't want this knowledge available to the public. Drunvalo recently reported that six more codices have been recovered. These ancient Mayan records reveal what has happened in the past during similar dimensional shifts, the last one taking place around 13,000 years ago. This information will be shared with the world.[17]

The Mayans talk about a transformation of humanity into something greater, a new way of being. In this new state we will learn to view the world in a different way. The Mayans do not believe the world is separate from our consciousness, much like the Chief has taught. They believe that consciousness shapes reality.

According to the Mayans, somewhere within the Seven-Year Window Earth's quarantine will be lifted. Once again we will be free to travel the universes. They intimate that after the shift in consciousness, when we regain our status as fully conscious beings, we won't need technology. We will be able to use our innate abilities to travel "without ships."

While the Mayans have many insights on our new beginning as a species, until recently they have been reluctant to speak about them openly. As Drunvalo reports, the Tibetans also know much about our ability to create our own universe consciously; but they will only discuss it after an individual has been through fourteen lifetimes with them.[18]

Prison Planet

Convincing humanity that we are a planet of sinful, ignorant, monkey-like beings has largely succeeded for thousands of years. To accomplish this, most of the evidence confirming our "divine heritage" has been destroyed. Myriad Star-Nations have come to watch our transition from limited beings into fully conscious ones. They speak of us as "genetic royalty." But ironically, a number of people still laugh and make jokes about little green men when extraterrestrial life is mentioned. This is shortly to end.

After a great cataclysm on Earth thousands of years ago, a group of rogue beings came here from the planet Nibiru seeking a world to exploit. Some of these beings became the ruling families of Atlantis. Others arrived from Orion, attracted by Earth's vast supply of resources, mainly gold.

These assorted beings, named in history as the Anunnaki, committed heinous crimes against the simple humans who were living on the surface of the Earth. Most of the more advanced humans had gone underground, to the Hollow Earth, prior to the cataclysm.

For centuries these powerful beings plundered the planet and terrorized its inhabitants. With their superior technology, they were able to manipulate the DNA of the humans. To this day, only two of the twelve strands of DNA are active. By tampering with humanity's genetics, they were able to create a more docile, animal-like, slave race.

Marduk, Enlil, Enki, Ea, and An were some of the major players in this drama. They openly exploited the Earth and ruled with little or no regard for other life-forms. They were looked upon as gods because they had abilities far beyond those of dumbed-down humans. They lived for centuries, and learned the secrets of time.

These black magicians created havoc up and down our timeline. According to Almine Barton, perhaps the worst perpetrator was, and still is, the being known as Thoth.[19] Ashayana Deane reports that Thoth once reached the pinnacle of spiritual mastery, but then succumbed to the lure of the dark side.[20] (It should be noted, however, that others revere the being known as Thoth and don't share in this view.)

The Anunnaki mated with selective humans and created a hybrid race to do their bidding while they were creating mischief elsewhere. These "Illuminati" bloodlines have ruled the planet for thousands of years. Until recently, their names were unknown, unlike those of their minions, who belong to secret societies like "Skull and Bones" and the "Bilderbergers." But within the Seven-Year Window, their devious machinations will be revealed and the perpetrators brought to justice.

The Anunnaki constructed a frequency fence around the planet using their advanced technology to keep their spoils to themselves. But the Higher Galactic Councils likely used the quarantine to keep the chaos on Earth from spilling over into the rest of the galaxy.

Because the Anunnaki and their minions ruled Earth, other Galactic Civilizations approaching the planet had to go through them. Help for humanity has been turned away time and again because the Anunnaki wished to run Earth as their private prison. Attempts to rescue humanity from their captors were met with threats of annihilation of their human shields.

The Anunnaki's blood kin, the Illuminati, carried out the day-to-day business. Their main goal was total global domination by the year 2000. But in 1995, according to Sheldan Nidle, everything changed. [This is but one of several different scenarios for the finale of the End Times movie.]

The experiment in polarity in our galaxy pitted the light against the dark. For the light to expand in wisdom, it needed the dark to resist it. At some point in our dim and misty past, representatives from both sides met and forged a divine prophecy: At the right time, a special declaration by Anchara, the dark lord, was to greatly transform this galaxy. The declaration was to terminate the galactic wars that had raged from one end of the Milky Way to the other, lasting millions of years.

"The Peace of Anchara" would have another benefit. It had the power to bring former foes together. This Treaty was to flood the galaxy with a new light, a light of Oneness and expanded consciousness. Nidle relates that this proclamation happened in 1995. At that time, the Anunnaki abandoned their plans for world control and withdrew from the planet.[21]

This left the various factions of the Illuminati and their minions in disarray. But rather than follow the lead of their masters, they squared off amongst each other to see who would head the One World Order. David Wilcock has been covering the final struggle to defeat the Illuminati on his website, *www.DivineCosmos.com*. The financial theater has become the primary battleground, but an elaborate plan by the light has now moved into the latter stages. Wilcock notes that a Divine Intervention is now in progress. He has chronicled a number of events confirming this in his excellent articles.[22]

With major events lining up for the timeframe surrounding 2012, the Earth, Herself, decided that a few of her wayward children would no longer be allowed to interfere with the evolution of humanity.[23] Furthermore, nuclear war would never again be tolerated on her surface. The Heavenly Councils supported this request, and decreed that humanity will have every opportunity to awaken and thereby move forward with the planet into the higher dimensions. At least in this version of the script, the rule of the dark appears to be ending.

As the Chief predicted, the old is crumbling before our very eyes. Once the media is free from the control of the Illuminati, "a world without secrets" will air. Needless to say, viewers will be shocked. Only those who have ventured down the rabbit hole will have been privy to the brilliant lies, the incredible secrecy, the cunning diversions, the bribery, debauchery, murder, and the genocide by the so-called "elite."

Some estimate that our evolution has been set back at least a hundred years. By this time we should have been living a space-age life like the Jetsons; disease should have been eradicated in the 20s; free energy and communication should also have been ours decades ago; global pollution should be nonexistent; world hunger eradicated; we could be teleporting across the planet and traveling throughout the galaxy. We could be getting our food from "light replicators" instead of grocery stores! But the rulers of the planet wanted something else. They wanted everything for themselves and nothing for the masses.

But, of course, that was the script the dark players were following. How will the audience react when the villains are unmasked? Will they recognize the dark ones as aspects of themselves? Time will tell. . . .

Awakening Humanity

Besides divine intervention, and the work of many courageous individuals working behind the scenes to secure our freedom, much credit for humanity's awakening must go to the Internet. Without it we might never have heard about Alex Collier's interaction with the Andromedans, David Icke's exposé of the global elite, or the testimony from Black Ops whistleblowers on

Project Camelot. Countless others have expanded our awareness, as well, and therefore our world. The truth is, we can only create and project a universe within the scope of our belief system.

When Columbus landed in the New World he was surprised to discover that the native people couldn't see his clipper ships. They were unable to see the big ships because they didn't know that big ships existed! The Nina, Pinta, and Santa Maria were floating in plain sight right off their shoreline.[24]

Until Columbus' arrival in 1492, the islanders of Hispaniola had never seen nor heard of large ocean-going vessels. "Ships" in their view of the world were limited to their tiny canoes. But once this knowledge had been added to their belief system and they were taught to "see" the big ships, the vessels appeared in their bay as if by magic.

It takes only a few visionaries to upgrade the entire group consciousness of a people. In the case of the natives, once a small number had learned about the new addition to their reality, the idea spread quickly through the group consciousness. Miraculously, everyone could then see the ships after that. To translate this into "Holographic Movie" terms: a few can change the script for the many.

For every one person who wakes up, it in turn affects 100,000 others around them. This "Hundredth Monkey Effect" tipped humanity's view of the world in March of 2012. The people woke up and "saw" that their leaders were enslaving them. The script was changed!

Clif High monitors language on the Internet and predicts trends based on his interpretation of the data coming through from the subconscious of humanity.

On March 9, 2012, he reported on his website that he believed the "KONY 2012" video had been watched by that final human that would be required to shift the planet. He points out that "release language" dominates from that point forward. This essentially means that "The Powers That Be," or as he calls them, "The Powers That Were," have lost in their bid for global dominance.[25]

David Wilcock wrote in his March article, "Divine Intervention: Defeating Financial Tyranny," that "massive, unprecedented ET interventions are completely disrupting any and all plans to start World War III." This information came from a number of inside sources. By March of 2012 the game had definitely changed.[26]

Another indication that March was indeed the tipping point came when Gaia, herself, sent a message to the Creator that she was now ready to move forward with the changes. She felt that, at long last, enough of humanity was prepared to proceed with the next steps in the awakening process.[27] It was time to step out of the shadows and return to the spotlight of galactic society.

*   *   *

"That I feed the hungry, forgive an insult,
and love my enemy . . . these are great virtues.
But what if I should discover that the poorest of the
beggars and the most impudent of offenders are all
within me, and that I stand in need of the alms of my
own kindness; that I myself am the enemy
who must be loved? What then?"

—Carl Jung
*Memories, Dreams,
Reflections* (1961)[28]

-12-

A Tale of Two Timelines

St. Germaine called it the "Golden Nebula,"[1] David Icke, the "Photon Belt;"[2] to others it is the "Photon Band." But another name exists for this spectacular band of multi-dimensional light that some say we are about to enter. This secret name is said to honor a powerful group of benevolent beings[3] now obscured by the mists of time, but once revered throughout the Milky Way Galaxy for their courage and integrity. It is called the "Dragon's Breath."

In *Voyagers II: Secrets of Amenti,* Ashayana Deane writes about Earth's "Stellar Activation Cycles," which occur roughly every 13,000 years. These are sometimes called "ascension cycles." During this time our planetary stargates, similar to chakras in the body, open and then align with the Galactic and Universal stargates.

When these alignments happen, the planetary population has the opportunity to move up in dimensional frequency. According to Deane, during a Stellar Activation Cycle, the planet's magnetic shields can hold the full "Dimension-12, Universal Maharata Creation Current," or "Pre-Matter Christos Current." This is also known as the "Holographic Beam," or the "Photon Belt."[4]

Alignment with this powerful current allows Earth to regenerate and realign with the Divine Template.

The Chief pegged the beginning of a new Golden Age to our entrance into this highly charged band. He would have enjoyed reading about the complex mechanics of this occurrence in the *Voyagers* book. Deane also says that on December 21, 2012, Earth's passage into the Photon Belt begins. On this date, Earth's magnetic and electrical poles reverse, as do Tara's (Earth's Fifth-Dimensional Body). Earth's grids then merge with Tara's. This "dimensional bridge" is sustained until the grids separate again in 2017.[5]

This is a simplified version of the process, but it may be that individuals whose vibrations are high enough will be able to stay in the Tara frequency when the grids separate. This would fulfill the description of "ascension," one of the End Times prophecies that is popular. Of course, others predict a much different ending—destruction.

Alternate Endings

Thoughts become things. In other words, our reality is molded by our beliefs. Those wishing to control the planet have used this simple truth against us. For this reason, controlling the flow of information through both television and the printed media has been prized from the beginning. A few wealthy individuals and their corporations have been influencing how the world is shaped. We have unwittingly imprisoned ourselves in their dark reality. Generating fear, their "energetic food," is the underlying agenda. An apocalypse of destruction is their ultimate aim.

But with the advent of the Internet, different, more liberating, ideas have been transforming our consensus reality. The movie script has been wrested from the hands of those who want devastation and chaos. An alternate, joyful finale has now been created.

When alternate endings first became popular, I wondered if there was a correlation between the movie industry and our reality matrix. If so, then there would likely be an opportune moment when a split in time would occur. It would probably happen during a pivotal scene near the end of the movie. The scene would need to be charged with suspense; fortunes would hang in the balance, perhaps lives; even the savviest of moviegoers would be left guessing about the outcome. The split could happen at any major juncture during the Seven-Year Window, but December 21, 2012, seems like the perfect time for the ultimate cliffhanger.

What would happen should we find ourselves crossing timelines? What would we experience upon waking in the morning? In all likelihood we would find life pretty much the same as the day before. The people that we work with would all show up on time; the market down the block would still sell flowers out front; the cat would still meet us at the bedroom door in the morning asking for food.

Remember, each of us is creating and projecting the universe that we experience. The people in our lives would likely "stay in character." In our universe, Joe, who drives our bus, would not mysteriously disappear and be replaced by an unknown driver. Joe would continue to play the role we had asked him to play.

In the event of a "subtle" timeline split, however, we might find that we are transferred to a more lucrative job in Orlando where we purchase a new car. We would no longer interact with Joe. The choices we make at crossroads in our lives might trigger such a shift without our conscious knowledge.

Splits may be more easily recognizable when events shift on the world stage. Few people are aware that a split happened the day Nelson Mandela was released from prison. When I met a friend named Daniel at the coffee shop, he had a bewildered look on his face. He blurted out that the strangest thing had happened to him that morning. I chimed in that I had experienced something very odd, too. It had left me reeling. Before I could elaborate, Daniel broke in, "Let me guess, did it have something to do with Nelson Mandela being released from prison?"

"Yes," I answered solemnly. "Nelson Mandela was supposed to die in prison." Daniel nodded in agreement. "There must have been a timeline split," he finally responded. "I wonder what *that* means?"

I'm guessing that Daniel would notice if there was a really big split, but I wonder how many others would be that aware? Did a split occur when 9/11 happened in 2001? It's likely, but I don't know for sure. Will anyone notice if a big shift in timelines happens in 2012? Can we influence which timeline we end up on? Will there be one exclusive outcome after the December 21, 2012, convergence?

Bill Woods, a whistleblower who appeared as a guest on Project Camelot, reported that he had worked on a "timeline project" for the government elite. Woods said that he had narrowed all possible scenarios down to two timelines, running parallel throughout the year 2012. The problem he was asked to solve was of great importance to those in power. They wanted to retain control of their "dark matrix" beyond 2012, but in every single model they had used, their plans for global control had failed.[6]

This is extremely significant. Even those choosing to continue their experiences here in the third dimension will have the luxury of doing so without the interference of the global elite!

It was never revealed what the "winning," positive scenario might be. We can only speculate that it involves a mass awakening and/or a dimensional shift. But we do have some clues about the two major timelines in question, the two different endings to the current movie. (It should be noted, however, that each of these timelines could have several minor variants.)

Timeline B

According to Drunvalo Melchizedek, Russian scientists have broken the "Crop Circle Code" and can now read them like we read a newspaper. He estimates that at least 20 per cent of the crop circles are legitimate, meaning, of extra terrestrial origin. No less than fifty scientists in Russia are actively participating in an esoteric project aimed at deciphering and disseminating the crop circle messages.[7]

As a caveat, it should be understood that ETs fall into both the Service-to-Others and the Service-to-Self categories. While, at a glance, some of the prophecies appear fear-based, a plan to mitigate these changes is also given. This suggests that positive ETs have been helping us; but, as usual, discretion is advised.

The messages state that seven different calamities are coming to Earth should we fail to awaken and clean

up our planet. Drunvalo states that the first one predicted by the crop circles is a solar flare that fries the
electrical grid and shuts down computers. As a worst-
case scenario, the scientists speculate that a magnetic
pulse of this magnitude could erase every computer
disc on Earth.[8]

If this should occur, those finding themselves on
this timeline—Timeline B—must begin to move up in
consciousness to the fourth dimension. According to
the messages, those who are unable to do so will find
it difficult to survive as the cleansing of the Earth pro-
gresses. The Russian scientists who are recommending
this change in consciousness are fully backed by their
government. Drunvalo revealed only one other catas-
trophe. That was the fourth, a physical pole shift.[9]

Undoubtedly more information will be forthcoming
prior to the first potential problem. The word "potential" is used here, for we all live in our own holographic
universe. This sequence of events may only transpire
in the reality of the scientists, and in the holograms of
those drawn to their work. Furthermore, experiencing
the drama of a pole shift may be what some individuals choose. Death is but a transition. Opportunities to
advance into higher dimensions with the planet will be
available from the other side, as well.

But shifting consciousness is a good idea no matter
what reality we find ourselves in. Moving from the head
to the heart is the key in every scenario. It is mainly
modern man who has fallen into the trap of living in
his head. He has lost his connection with Nature and
its Source. Indigenous people around the world already
seem to have this ability to "think from their heart."

When Carl Jung, the famous Swiss psychologist, met a Pueblo Chief named Ochwiay Biano, he found that he "could talk with him as he had rarely been able to talk with a European."

The Chief said he didn't understand the "Whites;" they were always restless, always seeking something with their furrowed faces and cruel, thin lips. The Chief confided to Jung that his people thought they were all mad.

When Jung pressed the Chief about this, he was told that the Whites "think with their heads."

"Why of course," Jung replied. "What do you think with?"

"We think here," replied the Chief, pointing to his heart![10]

Drunvalo explains that modern man needs to "connect the heart and the brain." He teaches this process in his workshops.[11] Drunvalo claims that most people can "remember" how to reconnect with their heart within five days. His method goes back to the Vedas, six thousand years ago.

It begins with letting go of anger and resentment, forgiving both others and ourselves. We must accept all parts of ourselves and begin loving every part. Once we are living in the heart, we can then connect with the heart of Mother Earth, the heart of the Sun, and the heart of the Universe. According to Drunvalo, Mother Earth has stated that anyone who does this will have nothing to worry about. They will survive any changes.[12]

Timeline A

At one time I used to put my attention on prophecies of doom and gloom. Admittedly, some part of me

183

was attracted to the drama. But fortunately, that fascination ran its course. For the past several years another finale has drawn my interest, one of an awakening humanity, a dimensional shift, and a golden future.

Rumors of a "Golden-Age Script" began to surface in the mid 90s. A few were talking about it back then, but the possibility of ending war, eliminating poverty, and curing disease was sheer fantasy to most. The corporate media had a stranglehold on the sleeping masses. But little by little people began to see through the lies and propaganda. 9/11 was a huge catalyst, a wake-up call. Rather than shock people into submission, it shook them awake. The alarm sounded, and was broadcast worldwide on the Internet.

Unbeknownst to most, a global financial war has been raging. A plan to free humanity from the debt-based system imposed on the world by illuminati bankers has quietly reached a critical juncture. Only recently have we heard about a new global financial system backed by commodities and precious metals. It will come online once the changes are rolling. Like in any good movie, the villains will be unmasked, much to the delight of the audience.

The plans of the Cabal, the Illuminati, were grandiose. Fortunately, they have been thwarted. The Illuminati were intent on murdering several billion people and enslaving the rest. To accomplish this, they seized control of several major governments, their militaries, the media, and many multinational corporations. The international bankers have planned and staged our biggest wars for the sole purpose of making money and furthering their global takeover.

These nefarious bankers were able to gain control of the world's gold supply by convincing the nations they had devastated that the only way to end war was to surrender their gold to a common pool; the international bankers would provide oversight, of course! Despite what they said or signed, they never intended to stop waging war, and they never intended to give back the gold.[13] After years of abuse, the nations of the world came together and decided that enough was enough. One by one they bought into "The Plan." They would bankrupt the bankers and their corporate holdings. The only countries opposed to the plan were those controlled by the Illuminati.

Lawsuits documenting the illegalities and crimes perpetrated by the Federal Reserve and the BIS have recently been filed. Concurrently, plans are moving forward for the arrests of thousands of government officials, bankers, and corporate heads. The details surrounding the multi-faceted and highly secretive plan to take back our freedom will one day be broadcast to the world. The script calls for televised arrests and the subsequent trials, debt forgiveness, and the implementation our new financial system.[14]

After the high profile arrests of politicians who sold out their people, those spearheading the global changes will appoint an interim government in the U.S. After six months, free and fair elections will be held to seat a new one. Sovereignty will be returned to the people of the restored Republic of the United States. An era of global abundance will begin.

Timeline A is also packed with revelations about our true history. Those labeled as "conspiracy nuts" will find redemption. The elite have been masters of conspiracy. To muddy the waters surrounding events such as 9/11, for instance, they create as many as eight different versions of the storyline.

Besides the truth about 9/11, the history behind the gold heist, and the release of countless inventions that could have liberated us from the oil, gas, and electric cartels decades ago, perhaps the biggest shock will be the extraterrestrial cover up. Not far behind the announcements of the new financial system and debt forgiveness, will come the event many have been waiting on for years—the Disclosure Scene.

The announcements will proclaim, "We are not alone;" in fact, we have never been alone. Countless ET races have visited Earth in the past. Many Service-to-Others ETs have returned to assist us in our transition to a higher state. After the initial announcements about our connection with myriad ET races, the first extraterrestrial humans will be introduced. These will include the Pleiadians, Sirians, and Andromedans. Other, "less-human" ETs will follow, once the initial shock has subsided.

For centuries the Agarthans have represented the planet in Galactic Councils. Not since the sinking of Atlantis over ten thousand years ago has there been a unified Earth. As the planetary vibrations have increased, and as humanity has begun to awaken, the Agarthans have made public their plans for a long overdue reunion with their surface cousins.

The Golden-Age Timeline is sometimes called the "Ascension Timeline." The defining event is a dimensional shift. People floating off and disappearing into clouds is fun to imagine, but realistically a shift in consciousness is much more subtle. We don't have to "go" anywhere. It's like tuning the radio dial in to a slightly different frequency and receiving an entirely new signal. Both frequencies coexist, although our senses can detect only one at a time. The higher dimensions are right here; the "New Earth" is here now! We can't detect it yet because we're still tuned in to the old paradigm. The dimensional shift will change the station for us.

When I was in my early twenties I experienced a rather unexpected shift. After my dentist had extracted a wisdom tooth, he instructed me to go home, take some pain medication, and lie down on the couch. It was the first time I'd taken strong pain pills, and by 6:00 p.m. I was feeling quite sociable. I decided to go see a football game at the high school.

As I was crossing the practice field, my consciousness suddenly got brighter. My surroundings transformed before my very eyes. The sky turned an iridescent blue. People walked by dressed in electric colors. The grass beneath me turned the brightest green I'd ever witnessed. Every blade was on fire, bursting with life. I marveled at the transformation. It lasted only a moment, but it altered my view of the world considerably.

The Mayans believe that everyone, at least those on this timeline, will experience the dimensional shift *en masse*. They say we have gone through similar shifts before, and will remember again when the time arrives. We carry the memory of these shifts in our heart. Help in making this transition will also come from Inner Earth and our galactic neighbors.

In preparation for this cosmic event, our bodies are going through many transformations. Low-frequency emotions, such as guilt, fear, and anger, are coming to the surface to be examined and then released. Crystalline cells cannot hold the negativity of carbon-based cells. A laundry list of symptoms has accompanied these upgrades. "Ascension symptoms" include dizziness, mental fog, body aches, depression, exhaustion, blurred vision, and countless others.

After we've made the shift, Drunvalo believes we will only be in the fourth dimension for about two years. We will then move on to the fifth dimension, where full consciousness awaits.[15] Our original, 12-strand DNA will have been restored by that time. In this awakened state there is no disease, no aging, and no need to labor at a mundane job. We can manifest whatever we desire at will; we can go wherever we wish unencumbered. There is no negativity to contend with, as we are beyond duality.

At this level of life we are sovereign cosmic citizens. We create with joy and wisdom, loving all that we create. Initially, the Agarthans and advanced galactic civilizations will be our teachers, since they have already ascended to this state. Then we will mentor others. Our contentious experiences with the dark polarity have made us sought after teachers throughout the universe.

Drunvalo reports that our ultimate destiny will take us beyond the twelfth dimension. What is happening here on Earth has never happened anywhere else in the universe. Earth is the key to a new creation. We are going to give birth to an entirely new universe, at a higher level, beyond anything we can imagine.[16]

Timeline A and Timeline B appear to be running side-by-side right now; but at some point, a discernible split should occur. As mentioned earlier, Andrew

Basiago said that participants in Project Pegasus, the time-travel project, reported that nothing could be seen past the date of December 21, 2012. After hearing that, I began considering alternatives to the two prominent timelines. I jokingly told a friend that perhaps the movie ends, the lights come on, and everyone walks out of the theater into Reality.

Dreams of the Paa Tal

According to the Andromedans, through their contactee, Alex Collier, the Souls populating Earth and twenty-one other star systems belong to an advanced group of beings called the "Paa Tal." The Andromedans say that the Paa Tal, also called the "Founders Race," came down from 11th Density to play in 3rd Density.[17]

Collier relates that the Andromedans say the Paa Tal created 3rd Density. Prior to this, they had been operating from 5th Density, after evolving up to the 11th trillions of years ago. Furthermore, the Andromedans say that we are living in a 21 trillion year-old hologram. Their history notes that this "level of the game" was conceived by *us*. We set up the ideas of free will and self-expression. For this reason, many of the benevolent ET races have been urging us to ask for help in waking up.[18]

The Andromedans believe that God has intervened and has made the decision to change the game. Perhaps He believes that the game has gotten out of hand, or that we have learned all that we need from our sojourn in duality.

The Andromedans know that everything in the universe came out of black holes, including us. They believe we are ageless, truly infinite. Collier's

Andromedan contacts, Morenae and Vissaeus, reported that on March 23, 1994, a specific color and sound
frequency began to emanate from all the black holes in
the known universe. This is the first time this has ever
happened, according to their extensive and ancient
records. The Andromedans believe that this new frequency is lifting everything up, birthing a new density—the 12th. The Andromedans say that by December
of 2013, 3rd Density will cease to exist.[19]

The Mayan Code

There is a Mayan greeting, a statement of oneness,
called *In Lak'ech Ala K'in*. When two people meet on
the path, this greeting is exchanged in honor of the
spirit within. It means "I am another you, and you are
another me." This simple concept translates into a code
of respect and recognition of Unity. It encompasses
living from the heart. As in other greetings, like *na-
maste* from South India, *Wiracocha* for the Inca, and
Mitakuye Oyasin for the Lakota, the hands are always
placed over the heart.[20]

When speaking about the realization of Oneness,
Hazrat Inayat Khan observed: "Man does not say of
his friend, 'This is my friend, I love him,' but says,
'This is myself, I love him.'"[21] Dr. Hew Len's practice of
Ho'oponopono reflects this understanding, as well. The
philosophy of *In Lak'ech Ala K'in* leads us away from
separateness, and into Oneness. It leads away from fear
and into the awareness that the essence of all things is
love. We can extend this greeting to trees, animals, our
planet, and the stars, for all are interconnected.[22] In
truth, one spirit moves through everything.

Living in the spirit of *In Lak'ech Ala K'in* translates into giving from the heart—appreciation, love, and respect. It means taking positive action, rather than being neutral; it means changing the script in a positive manner, rather than complaining about negativity.[23]

Each moment we have a choice: will it be love or will it be fear? By opening the heart we will no longer focus on disaster. Instead, we will manifest a glorious future. The Mayans say we will come together as "one living being."[24] A life of beauty, joy, freedom, and abundance will flow into form without conscious effort. It will emanate from the center of the world, our own heart.

*   *   *

I packed a few things in my car and glanced wistfully at the coffee shop as I left town one rainy Friday evening. Where would I go? Usually I gravitated to Colliding Rivers at turning points in my life, but not today. Perhaps I'd drive to the beach. It was nice having freedom of choice.

But why the Pacific? Was it calling me for a reason? Would I return a changed person, I wondered? Was I finally ready to face the third challenge, to reach for that star? There were plenty of questions to pick from, but one stood out . . . and the answer to that one was readily apparent: Had I known at an earlier age that One Spirit surged through everything, would I have lived my life differently? No doubt about it.

I flipped on the radio and, to my surprise, a song was playing that I'd never heard before. It was synchronistically appropriate. A fresh, new cycle was just beginning. Yes, the beach felt right. It was vast, unpredictable, mysterious. The Chief would approve.

A line from "Star Trek VI: The Undiscovered Country" came to mind. Chekov was asking for a heading. Captain Kirk gazed out upon the galaxy with an appreciative smile:

"Second star to the right, Mr. Chekov, and straight on till morning"[25]

Surrendering the River

The ninth wave is the largest, most powerful, most respected, and the most sublime of all waves. But it faces an unsolvable problem. By now the ashes of the Chief have reached the shores of the vast Pacific after joining earlier with the Umpqua. No doubt the Chief's spirit has already been called upon for advice.

The Unsolvable Problem

As the ninth wave crested, a sadness arose deep within its heart. It realized that its identity as "wave" would soon be coming to an end. All its life it had struggled to become the biggest, the best, and the longest to survive. Someday, if it worked hard enough, the ninth wave felt that it would be worthy enough to be accepted by Ocean.

It was the illusion of separateness that had created the ninth wave's identity. But it had also created a "veil of forgetfulness." You see, at the time of separation, the wave forgot that it had always been Ocean. At separation the desire to get somewhere, to accomplish something, to achieve some goal, had been born. The wave

193

longed for greatness; but deep in its heart it longed for something that it thought could never be achieved. It longed to be Ocean.

But to return to its origin required dropping the wave's very identity. "Separate" is how the wave viewed itself. All its life it had struggled to maintain its separateness, its identity. Its survival depended upon it. How could it conceive of dropping *itself*? It was an unsolvable problem.

I can hear the Chief's calm voice echoing through the turbulent surf as he shares what he has learned from his own journey. The ninth wave listens intently.

JR: "My friend," the Chief offered, "you must cease all struggling, for struggling will result in only your frustration. To drop the illusion of being separate is impossible, for separateness is your very nature. To reach the level of Ocean there is nothing to do, nothing to achieve, nothing to attain. You see, waves cannot reach the level of Ocean through any effort of their own.

"There is but one solution to the unsolvable problem: Surrender. Once a wave does this, it will instantly find itself at the level of Ocean where there is blissful existence."

Surrendering Identity

M: Overlooking the shimmering Pacific from a sand dune near the confluence of the Umpqua, I can clearly hear the Chief's soft voice in rhythm with the tides. In his kind manner, he is sharing with the wave the river's struggle for survival.

JR: "Where the mighty North Umpqua greets the Pacific at the end of its long and many-faceted journey, there is a joining. It's not the first time the river has experienced this. It once merged with Little River; indeed, many of its soft qualities had come from that joining. But it was Little River that had surrendered its identity that day. It could no longer broadcast to the world, 'I AM Little River.'

"When it was the Umpqua's turn to face a crisis of survival, trepidation ran through its green-blue currents, for it knew that no force on Earth could stave off its inevitable fate. In moments it would lose the struggle it had always fought—survival. No longer would it be able to say, 'I AM Umpqua.'

"The shift came in an instant. To the mighty river's shock, when the dreaded moment came there was a deep and joyous peace. In the reality of 'Ocean' it surrendered its dream of being 'River.' Both its separateness and its struggle to survive vanished instantly in the vastness of the sea. River realized that being separate had been the source of all its problems. Only by surrendering its struggle to survive could it awaken into 'existence.'"

The Call to Awaken

M: Through the last light of day I can see gulls searching for scraps along the deserted beach, now at low tide. Their lives are consumed by a constant struggle for survival. Aside from an occasional squabble over food, a calm has settled over the restless sea. In the Chief's familiar tone I hear the Breath of All Life form Itself into words.

All That Is: "In the mists of the waterfall I have called to thee, Dear One: 'Surrender your cares.' In the voices of a hundred streams that feed the Umpqua I have called to thee: 'Surrender, come home.' With the

195

churning voice of the river I have beckoned thee, Oh Soul: 'Surrender now your salmon-filled streamlets.' As Ocean, I called to thee again: 'Surrender ye the river with its lifetimes rich with memories.' Despite myriad illusions and powerful resistance, you have found your way here.

"Once more, Dear Heart, I call to thee with love: 'Surrender now the vastness of the rolling sea. Surrender and awaken. Your true home awaits thee, beyond the thought of oceans, beyond the ken of continents. This home has no identity, no beliefs, no struggles, no limitations. It harbors no illusions, no beginnings, and no endings, only dreams to be dreamed with never-ending joy. Surrender now, Beloved, for awakening from Dreamland requires only this.'"

*   *   *

The dreams that we surrender on the break
bring us back to Ocean wide awake.

Acknowledgments

Special thanks to Jamie Davis for sharing his waking dreams with me over the years, and to Marie Eklund for contributing valuable reference material for this book.

I would also like to thank Karla McMechan, my editor, who worked long hours researching, editing, and polishing this book. Her attention to detail greatly improved the Notes section in particular. Robin McBride, my typesetter, was a joy to work with. I heartily recommend her company, RMcB Creative Services, for all aspects of book design and publishing. She may be contacted through her website at *www.rmcbcreative.com*, or by phone at (541) 603-1335.

I extend my heartfelt gratitude to Alorah Melchizedek for her support and encouragement during the writing process. She scanned the Internet for suitable cover graphics, sent me quotes to review for chapter endings, and took the time to read through selected parts of the manuscript and offer content suggestions. Our discussions of the hologram, timelines, and ascension provided inspiration that shifted this book. Her energetic "Colour Matrix Essences" are sold worldwide: *www.ColourMatrixEssences.com*.

Notes

Preface

1. Michael Harrington, *Touched by the Dragon's Breath: Conversations at Colliding Rivers* (Susan Creek Publishing, 2005), *www.SusanCreek.com.*

2. Michael Avery, *The Secret Language of Waking Dreams* (Eckankar, 1992).

Introduction

1. Michael Harrington, *Porcupines at the Dance: Parables and Stories from Colliding Rivers* (Susan Creek Publishing, 2008).

PART I: PERCHANCE TO DREAM

Chapter 1: Stan, Stan, the Bigfoot Man

1. Henry David Thoreau, *Walden, and Other Writings* (Random House, 1992) p. 85.

2. Harrington, *Dragon's Breath,* Chapter 4: Secrets of Creation, pp. 41–57.

3. Michael Talbot, *The Holographic Universe* (HarperPerennial, 1992) p. 141.

4. Edgar Allan Poe, poem, "A Dream within a Dream," in *Complete Stories and Poems of Edgar Allan Poe* (Doubleday, 1984) p. 768. First published in 1849.

Chapter 2: Crossing Kaiulani

1. For example, the Vairagi mentioned by Paul Twitchell and others.

2. Paul Twitchell describes the Sound Current as "the divine being expressing ITSELF in something that is both audible and visible," *The Far Country* (Illuminated Way Press, 1971, 6th printing, 1978) p. 158.

   Hazrat Inayat Khan writes, "It sounds like thunder, the roaring of the sea, the jingling of bells, running water, the buzzing of bees, the twittering of sparrows, the vina, the whistle, the sound of shanka—until it finally becomes Hu, the most sacred of all sounds," *The Sufi Message of Hazrat Inayat Khan, Vol. II: The Mysticism of Sound* (Barrie & Jenkins, London, 1962, 1973) p. 64; and available online at *www.sufimessage.com.*

3. Pythagoras believed that the Music of the Spheres was produced by the vibration of the celestial spheres upon which he thought the stars and planets moved. For more information, see Paul A. Calter, "Pythagoras & Music of the Spheres," (Dartmouth College, 1998) on *www.dartmouth.edu / ~matc / math5.geometry / unit3 / unit3.html* and Khan, *Sufi Message*, Vol. II, "Music of the Spheres."

4. Direct experience with this wave or Sound Current is described by numerous adventurous Souls, often called "mystics," in and out of every spiritual path and religion.

5. Harrington, *Porcupines*, p. 54.

Chapter 3: Signs and Synchronicity

1. Ellie Crystal, "Carl Jung and Synchronicity," *www .crystalinks.com / synchronicity.html.*

2. I tell this story using the name "Stella" in "The Tree on the Stump," Avery, *The Secret Language,* pp. 11–12.

3. A similar telling of this story, "The Three White Eagles," appears in *The Secret Language,* pp. 68–70.

4. Willard A. Heaps, *Superstition!* (Thomas Nelson, 1972) p. 27.

5. Henry Foljambe Hall, *Napoleon's Letters to Josephine: 1796-1812* (E. P. Dutton & Co, 1901) p. 210.

6. This quote is very popular on the Internet, but I have yet to find its original source. It may well be in *Synchronicity: An Acausal Connecting Principle,* translated by R. F. C. Hull (Bollingen Series, Princeton University Press, copyright 1960, reissued in 2010). This quote is included in the very helpful library of quotes, arranged by subject and author, on the website of Giam Life: *blog.gaiam.com / quotes / authors / carl-jung.*

Chapter 4: Sedona

1. Harrington, *Dragon's Breath,* p. 91.

2. In 1985 the Wings of the Wind property was owned by Eckankar.

3. Avery, *Secret Language,* pp. 103–104, paraphrased.

4. Guillaume Apollinaire, *www.quotationsbook.com / quote / 14688.*

PART II: THE CHIEF'S FINAL DISCOURSES

Chapter 5: Invincibility of the Inner Warrior

1. Rick Keefe interviews Alex Collier, "First Alex Collier Video that Changed the World—1994." View at *www .youtube.com / watch?v=MLZJ-Snbkz8.*

2. The full version of Terry Dobson's story can be found in *Chicken Soup for the Soul* by Jack Canfield and Mark Victor Hansen (Health Communications, Inc., 1993) pp. 55–58. It was originally published in *Safe and Alive* (Putnam Publishing Group, 1982). I've taken the liberty of retelling the story in the third person.

3. *The Razor's Edge* by W. Somerset Maugham was first published in 1944. Its epigraph from the Katha-Upanishad reads: "The sharp edge of the razor is difficult to pass over; thus the wise say the path to Salvation is hard." The 1946 movie version of *The Razor's*

Edge starred Tyrone Power; the 1984 remake featured Bill Murray in one of his best performances.

4. "Morihei Ueshiba (1883–1969)" on *FightingMaster.com* [online martial arts publication edited by Gus Fant], Quotation #13 [on 9/3/2012], *www.fightingmaster.com/masters/ueshiba/quotes.htm*.

Chapter 6: The Dreamland Matrix

1. Lyall Watson, *Gifts of Unknown Things: A True Story of Nature, Healing, and Initiation from Indonesia's Dancing Island* (Destiny Books, 1991) pp. 202–204.

2. William Grimes, "Lyall Watson, 69, Adventurer and Explorer of the 'Soft Edges of Science,' Dies," *New York Times*, July 21, 2008, *www.nytimes.com/2008/07/21/science/21watson.html?_r=1&pagewanted=all*.

3. Tia's story is summarized and interpreted by Talbot in *Holographic Universe,* p. 155.

4. Watson, *Gifts of Unknown Things*, p. 203.

5. Paramahansa Yogananda, "Materializing a Palace in the Himalayas," Chapter 34, *An Autobiography of a Yogi, www.ananda.org/autobiography/#chap34*.

6. Walter Russell, *The Secret of Light* (University of Science and Philosophy, Third edition, 1947) p. 223. Also available as a free e-book on *http://archive.org/stream/WalterRussellThe SecretOfLight/WalterRussell_The SecretOfLight#page/n7/mode/2up*.

7. Russell, *Secret of Light,* p. 281.

8. Joe Vitale and Ihaleakala Hew Len, PhD, *Zero Limits* (John Wiley & Sons, 2007) p. 33.

9. Based on Jessica Mystic interview, "A Conversation with Andrew Basiago about the Hidden History of His Discovery of Life on Mars," 8/31/09. View at *www.youtube.com/watch?v=iwE8m50sbWk*. Andrew Basiago, a Black Ops whistleblower, reveals that, through his father's connections, he was recruited as a child into a secret time travel program called "Project Pegasus." In the 1960s his supervisors called our

holographic reality "The Matrix." (This was decades before the movie by the same name came out starring Keanu Reeves in 1999.)

10. Talbot's interpretation of Yogananda's quote in *Holographic Universe,* p. 153. Original quote from *Autobiography of a Yogi* (p. 134) reads: "The world [is] nothing more than an objectivized dream, says Yogananda, whatever your powerful mind believes very intensely immediately comes to pass."

Chapter 7: Birth of the *Sat Shatoiya*

1. Mark Hoy, "A History of Steamboat Inn & the Fly Fishing Tradition of the North Umpqua River," *www .thesteamboatinn.com / history_early.html.*

2. Joseph Campbell, *The Hero's Journey* (New World Library, 2003).

   Steps of the Hero's Journey are summarized at the Maricopa Center for Learning and Instruction website *www.mcli.dist.maricopa.edu / smc / journey / ref / summary.html.*

3. Chatoyancy is defined in "Gemstone Words and Terms Glossary" at *www.jewelry-design-gemstone.com / gemstone-words-glossary.html* as: "The appearance of well-defined bands or threads of light across the surface of a gemstone. This appearance is caused by the reflection of light off small parallel mineral inclusions." An example of a single-band chatoyancy is Cat's Eye; Tiger's Eye consists of a series of bands.

   I'd like to thank my friend, Shatoiya De La Tour, for sharing the information about the origin of her name with me. Her popular book, *Earth Mother Herbal,* can be found on Amazon.com.

4. Alice Bailey & Djwal Khul, *A Treatise on the Seven Rays*, Volume 2: Esoteric Psychology, Vol. II. (Lucis Trust, 1942).

5. The Fourth Ray is also called the Ray of Harmony through Conflict.

6. Paul Twitchell, *The ECK-Vidya* (Eckankar, 1972) pp. 43–45.

7. Paulo Coelho, *The Alchemist* (HarperCollins, 1988) p. 128.

Chapter 8: Farewell

1. Hazrat Inayat Khan, "Love" *Spiritual Message of Hazrat Inayat Khan*, Volume VIIIa (Sufi Teachings), Part IV (Love), *www.wahiduddin.net / mv2 / VIIIa / VIIIa_4_1.htm*.

2. Louise Hay, *You can Heal Your Life* (Hay House, 1984, 1987, 2004).

3. The hidden hand of the global elite may be the projected shadow of humanity's dark choices.

4. Khan, *Spiritual Message*, "Bowl of Saki for April 6, 2012," *www.wahiduddin.net / saki / saki_date.php ?month=4&day=6*.

PART III: A HOLOGRAPHIC VIEW OF THE END TIMES

Chapter 9: *Ho'oponopono*

1. Carl Jung, *BrainyQuotes.com*, *www.brainyquote.com / quotes / quotes / c / carljung146686.html*.

2. Vitale & Len, *Zero Limits,* p. 21. See also Ihaleakala Hew Len, "Who's in Charge?" *www.self-i-dentity -through-hooponopono.com / article9.htm*. In this article Dr. Len states: "I love Self Identity *Ho'oponopono* and dear Morrnah Nalamaku Simeona, Kahuna Lapa'au, who so graciously shared it with me in November, 1982."

3. Vitale & Len, *Zero Limits,* p. 24.

4. Vitale & Len, *Zero Limits,* p. 22.

5. Vitale & Len, *Zero Limits,* p. 6.

6. Vitale & Len, *Zero Limits,* p. 71.

7. Masaru Emoto, "The Clean Water Experiment," *www .youtube.com / watch?v=BsBjzU_k4DM*. Dr. Masaru Emoto's Lake Biwa event was a global Intention

Experiment to clean up polluted Lake Biwa on March 22, 2010.

8. Vitale & Len, *Zero Limits,* p. 41.

9. Len, "Who's in Charge?" *www.self-i-dentity-through -hooponopono.com / article9.htm.*

Chapter 10: Mt. Shasta and Inner Earth

1. Kerri Carpenter, "Auld Lang Syne and Film," *www .suite101.com / article / auld-lang-syne-and-film- a186306.*

   See also Maurice Lindsay, "Auld Lang Syne," The Burns Encyclopedia (New 3d edition), Robert Hale, Ltd., 1996, now online at *www.robertburns.org / encyclopedia / AuldLangSyne.5.shtml.*

2. This backstory is paraphrased from "About Mt. Shasta" and "About Lemuria and Telos," posted on *www .lemurianconnection.com*, founded by Aurelia Louise Jones.

   For more details, see *Telos* by Aurelia Louise Jones (3 volumes, Mt. Shasta Light Publishing, 2004–2006) and *Telos: Original Transmissions from the Subterranean City beneath Mt. Shasta* by Dianne Robbins (4th Edition, Trafford Publishing, 2008).

3. James Churchward, *The Lost Continent of MU* (Brotherhood of Life/BE Books, 1926) pp. 1, 6, 51.

4. Dianne Robbins, "Sharula Dux on Telos and Hollow Earth," August, 2007, *www.youtube.com / watch?v=H7mGQvM4VsY.* Sharula Dux is a princess from the subterranean city of Telos situated beneath Mt. Shasta, which is populated by the remnants of the Lemurian civilization.

   Much of the information provided by Sharula Dux can also be found at *www.lemurianconnection.com.*

   More on Telos and the Hollow Earth at *www .DianneRobbins.com* and *http://hollowplanet.blogspot .com.*

   Shamballa-the-Greater is on the etheric plane.

5. "Telos means Communication with Spirit, oneness with Spirit, understanding with Spirit." *www .lemurianconnection.com* in "About Lemuria and Telos."

6. For more information on Mt. Shasta and the city beneath it, see *www.lemurianconnection.com*. The article, "About Mt. Shasta," describes it as "embraced in a gigantic, etheric purple pyramid whose capstone reaches far beyond this planet into space. It connects us intergalactically to the Confederation of Planets for this sector of the Milky Way Galaxy. This awesome pyramid is also created as an inverted version of itself, reaching down to the very core of the Earth. You can call Mt. Shasta the entry point of the Light-Grids of this planet, where most of the energy comes first from the galactic and universal core before it is disseminated to other mountains and into the grids. . . . Strange lights and sounds are often seen or heard on the mountain." *www.lemurianconnection.com / category / about-mt-shasta /.*

7. Phylos, *A Dweller on Two Planets* (Borden Publishing Co., 1952).

8. Robbins, "Sharula Dux," Part 3.

9. Robbins, "Sharula Dux," Part 4.

10. Dianne Robbins, *Messages from the Hollow Earth* (Trafford Publishing, 2003) p. 90. See also *www .DianneRobbins.com*.

11. Robbins, "Sharula Dux," Part 7.

12. Robbins, "Sharula Dux," Parts 4, 5, 8.

13. Evidence suggests that our DNA has been compromised at different times in history by those wishing to control the surface world and its peoples. By severing the connection to our Higher Selves we've been easily controlled.

14. Robbins, "Sharula Dux," Part 11.

15. Robbins, "Sharul Dux," Part 5.

16. Robbins, "Sharula Dux," Part 6.

17. Robbins, "Sharula Dux," Parts 1, 2.

18. Robbins, "Sharula Dux," Part 3.

19. Dianne Robbins, *Telos,* (New Expanded Edition, Trafford Publishing, 2008) p. 25. See also *www .DianneRobbins.com.*

20. Robbins, *Hollow Earth,* p. 30.

21. Robbins, *Hollow Earth,* p. 15.

22. Robbins, *Hollow Earth,* p. 17.

23. Robbins, *Hollow Earth,* pp. 24–25.

24. Robbins, *Hollow Earth,* p. 27.

25. Robbins, *Hollow Earth,* pp. 26–27.

26. Robbins, *Hollow Earth,* pp. 28–29.

27. Robbins, *Telos,* p. 47.

Chapter 11: Event Horizon: Zero Point

1. John Neihardt, *Black Elk Speaks* (New York: University of Nebraska Press, 1972) p. 33.

2. Cited by Russell in *Secret of Light,* p. 212.

3. Our brain interprets the interference pattern of these frequencies and constructs our holographic reality.

4. Nassim Haramein, "Crossing the Event Horizon," recorded live at the Rogue Valley Metaphysical Library, Ashland, Oregon, June 13, 2006. View at *www.youtube.com / watch?v=N2qLIeN7gRI.*

5. Stuart Wilde, "Mirror World Theories" (February 8, 2012), *www.stuartwilde.com / 2012 / 02 / mirror-world -theories / .*

6. Alfred Webre interviews Drunvalo Melchizedek on 12/20/11, "Mayan End Time Prophecies of Earth Changes, Consciousness Transformation, and the Divine Feminine, 2007—Jan. 1, 2016." View at *www .youtube.com / watch?v=d8v03EVrvwI.*

7. Double toroid graphic from *http://cosmometry.net/ the-torus---dynamic-flow-process.* Illustration by Goa Lobaugh, Liquid Buddha Studios. With permission.

8. Harrington, *Dragon's Breath,* Introduction. There are 2,160 of these 104,000-year cycles in one 225-million-year Galactic Orbit.

9. David Icke, *The Biggest Secret* (Bridge of Love Publications, 1999) pp. 476–77.

   Terrance and Dennis McKenna collaborated on *The Invisible Landscape: Mind, Molecules, and the I Ching* (2nd Edition, HarperCollins, 1993). NOTE: A review of this book appears on Amazon that references "the holographic theory of the mind."

10. Andrew Hamilton, "Journey into a Schwarzschild black hole," included on the University of Colorado website at *http://jila.colorado.edu/~ajsh/insidebh/ schw.html*. Hamilton is a Professor of Astrophysical and Planetary Sciences of the University of Colorado, Boulder, Colorado.

11. Mystic, "A Conversation with Andrew D. Basiago," 8/31/09.

12. John Smallman, "Be prepared for mighty life-altering events to happen," *www.JohnSmallman.com*, archived on 4/8/12.

13. Webre, Melchizedek interview, "Mayan End Time Prophecies," 12/20/11.

14. Webre, Melchizedek interview, "Mayan End Time Prophecies," 12/20/11.

15. Webre, Melchizedek interview, "Mayan End Time Prophecies," 12/20/11.

16. Webre, Melchizedek interview, "Mayan End Time Prophecies," 12/20/11.

17. Webre, Melchizedek interview, "Mayan End Time Prophecies," 12/20/11. Drunvalo referred to the six recently recovered codices on 4/30/12 when he answered questions about ascension: *www.youtube.com/ watch?v=hWaeSAo7FY8*.

18. Webre, Melchizedek interview, "Mayan End Time Prophecies," 12/20/11.

19. Almine Barton, "Anunnaki Dark Gods/Thoth," 8/6/08, view at *www.youtube.com / watch?v=1AA4pW8QVLs &list=PL5BD39AEE73E8D0A6&index=13&feature= plpp_video.*

20. Deane, *Voyagers II,* p. 260.

21. Sheldan Nidle, *www.paoweb.com / sn101210.htm.*

22. See David Wilcock's blog articles on *www.DivineCosmos .com,* for example: "China October Surprise II: Earth's Quarantine Has Lifted, 26 November 2010," "Divine Intervention: ETs Defeating Old World Order, 09 May 2012," "Financial Tyranny: Defeating the Greatest Cover-Up of All Time, 13 January 2012," and "Mass Arrests: David Interviews Drake, 05 April 2012."

    Recently two new spokesmen have arrived on the scene: Drake, a point person for the positive military (*www.americannationalmilitia.com*), and Cobra, who represents the "Resistance Movement." Cobra's mission is to keep the public informed about the liberation of the planet and the removal of the Dark Cabal: *www.2012portal.blogspot.com.*

23. According to Ashayana Deane in *Voyager II,* Earth's name in the fifth dimension is Terra; in the dimension, Gaia, and in the twelfth, Aramatena.

24. In the film, "What the Bleep Do We Know (2004), Candace Pert, Ph.D., an internationally recognized pharmacologist, retold the story of the Hispaniola islanders. She began by saying, "We only see what we believe is possible. We match patterns that already exist within ourselves through conditioning." For the source of this story, see "Questioning perceptual blindness: I see no ships," by David Hambling, *Fortean Times: The World of Strange Phenomena,* February 2007, on *www.forteantimes.com / strangedays / science / 20 / questioning_perceptual_blindness.html.*

25. Clif High, "Conceptual Context Threshold," *www. halfpasthuman.com,* March 9, 2012.

26. Wilcock, "Divine Intervention, Section 1—Defeating Financial Tyranny," posted 28 March 2012 on *www .DivineCosmos.com*.

27. Wanderer of the Skies, a letter from the Federation dated March 24 2012, posted on *www.galacticchannelings .com / english / wanderer25-03-12*.

28. Carl G. Jung, *Memories, Dreams, Reflections,* included on *www.goodreads.com / work / quotes / 848877 -memories-dreams-reflections*.

Chapter 12: A Tale of Two Timelines

1. Mary Carroll Nelson, *Beyond Fear: A Toltec Guide to Freedom and Joy* (Council Oaks Books, 1997) p. 31.

   See also Allisone Heartsong, "Planetary Ascension Confirmed" Expanded version (In God We Trust, 2002) posted on *www.planetaryascension.net / Planetary_ascension / planetary_ascension.htm*.

   Heartsong writes, "In August 1987, the week of the Harmonic Convergence, the I AM Presence of ascended master Saint Germain, speaking through his dedicated full-body channel Azena, gave five public presentations in Mt. Shasta. . . . All five presentations were recorded . . . and key portions were later published by Triad in 1993 as chapters 4 through 6 of *Earth's Birth Changes [by Saint Germaine through channeler Azena Ramanda].* . . . Describing it as 'the physical manifestation of the Second Coming of Christus,' Sainte Germain declared: 'That which you call the golden nebula is the New Age perceived.' He then predicted that its approach will give rise to an exponential acceleration of synchronistic events as we gradually shift into higher frequencies of energy, adding: 'When you traverse this threshold, when you become one with the golden nebula, you are in superconsciousness.'"

2. Icke, *Biggest Secret,* pp. 476–77.

3. Ancient Order of Beneficent Dragons (from a contemplation by the author).

4. Deane, *Voyagers II,* p. 283.

5. Deane, *Voyagers II,* p. 220.

6. Kerry Cassady, Project Camelot: Bill Wood: Above and Beyond Project Looking Glass. View at *www.youtube.com / watch?v=nkIIBnIuXHM*, posted January 17, 2012.

7. Lilou Mace interviews Drunvalo Melchizedek on 4/7/12, "Crop Circles, Russians, coming solar flares . . . use your discernment!!" View at *www.youtube.com / watch?v=N46nqG07FN0.*

8. Mace, Melchizedek interview, "Crop Circles, Russians," 4/7/12.

9. Mace, Melchizedek interview, "Crop Circles, Russians," 4/7/12. The "Avebury 2008 Crop Circle," discussed in this interview, is among the most famous. It predicted a physical pole shift taking place around 2013/2014.

10. Jean Haines, "Jung in Conversation with a Native American Chief," *jhaines6.wordpress.com / 2011 / 04 / 19 / jung-in-conversation-with-a-native-american-chief /*; Jean writes that this story comes from Gail Godwin, *Heart, A Personal Journey through Its Myths and Meanings* (1st edition, William Morrow, 2001).

11. Drunvalo Melchizedek, "Awakening the Illuminated Heart," School of Remembering, *www.Drunvalo.net.* View description at *www.drunvalo.net / upcoming1.php.*

12. Webre, Melchizedek interview, "Mayan End Time Prophecies," 12/20/11.

13. David Wilcock interviews Winston Shrout, "Arrest Warrants: Liens filed against G7 Central Banks," 5/1/12, *www.divinecosmos.com / start-here / davids-blog / 1051-g7banks.* Interview also uploaded to *www.youtube.com / watch?v=nI3snh-V6Sw.*

14. Wilcock interviews Shrout, "Arrest Warrants: Liens filed against G7 Central Banks."

15. Drunvalo Melchizedek, "Q & A with Drunvalo: Episode 1," 4/30/12 *www.youtube.com / watch?v=3FjwHJraivc.*

16. Melchizedek, "Q & A," 4/30/12; also, Melchizedek, "Conversation with Cal Garrison," April 2012. Garrison is the editor of "Spirit of Ma'at Magazine," available at *www.drunvalo.net / videostore / index.php.*

17. Alex Collier, "The Paa Tal—Redoux," *Defending Sacred Ground*, chapter 1, available at *www.whale .to / b / collier.pdf.*

18. Alex Collier, "Our Universe is a Hologram," *Defending Sacred Ground*, chapter 1, available at *www.whale .to / b / collier.pdf.*

19. Collier, "Our Universe is a Hologram."

20. Aluna Joy Yaxk'in, "In Lak'ech Ala K'in—The Living Code of the Heart," *www.spiritlibrary.com / center -of-the-sun / in-lakech-ala-kin-the-living-code-of-the -heart.*

21. Hazrat Khan, *Sufi Message, Vol. II,* p. 133.

22. Yaxk'in, "Living Code of the Heart."

23. Yaxk'in, "Living Code of the Heart."

24. Webre, Melchizedek interview, "Mayan End Time Prophecies," 12/20/11.

25. I've taken liberties with a quote from another favorite movie, Walt Disney's Peter Pan, "Memorable Quotes from Peter Pan (1953), *www.imdb.com / title / tt0046183 / quotes.*

About the Author

Michael Harrington grew up near Colliding Rivers in southern Oregon. His early life revolved around sports, especially baseball, where he was named to the all-state team in high school as a shortstop. After finishing college, he worked briefly as a real estate developer with his brother before striking out on his own to pursue writing.

Michael's first success came in the early 80s when one of his children's books, *The Catbird's Secret*, was accepted by a large publisher. The project later fell through; but the experience yielded sufficient motivation to continue writing. In 1990 he wrote *The Secret Language of Waking Dreams*, a popular book on synchronicity (published in 1992 under a different name).

In 2005 Michael founded Susan Creek Books, named for a famous stream near Colliding Rivers. *Touched by the Dragon's Breath* came out that same year, followed by *Porcupines at the Dance* in 2008.

Besides writing, Michael enjoys perusing the Internet, socializing with friends, and exploring old-growth forests. His favorite trails lead to waterfalls strung out

like jewels along the many tributaries of the Scenic
North Umpqua River.